The
Underachieving
School

ALSO BY JOHN HOLT

How Children Fail
How Children Learn
What Do I Do Monday?
Freedom and Beyond
Escape from Childhood
Instead of Education
Never Too Late
Teach Your Own
Learning All the Time

The Underachieving School

John Holt

Foreword by
Patrick Farenga

SENTIENT PUBLICATIONS

Cover design by Kim Johansen
Book design by Timm Bryson

Library of Congress Cataloging-in-Publication Data

Holt, John Caldwell, 1923-1985
  The underachieving school / by John Holt.-- 1st Sentient
Publications ed.
      p. cm.
Originally published: Pitman Pub. Corp., 1969.
Includes bibliographical references.
ISBN 1-59181-038-8
1. Education--United States. 2. Education--Philosophy. I. Title.
LA217.H6 2005
370'.973--dc22

2005019421

For acknowledgments, see page 146.

Printed in the United States of America

10 9 8 7 6 5 4 3 2

SENTIENT PUBLICATIONS, LLC
1113 Spruce Street
Boulder, CO 80302
www.sentientpublications.com

Contents

QUESTION
(from the editors of *Education News*, New York City)
If America's schools were to take one giant step forward this year toward a better tomorrow, what should it be?

ANSWER
(from John Holt)
It would be to let every child be the planner, director, and assessor of his own education, to allow and encourage him, with the inspiration and guidance of more experienced and expert people, and as much help as he asked for, to decide what he is to learn, when he is to learn it. How he is to learn it, and how well he is learning it. It would be to make our schools, instead of what they are, which is jails for children, into a resource for free and independent learning, which everyone in the community, of whatever age, could use as much or as little as he wanted.

FOREWORD

FOR READERS OF A CERTAIN age all I have to do is write, "The United States of America, 1969" and all sorts of images, sounds, and thoughts enter their minds. For those unfamiliar with the period known as "The Sixties" there are more than enough histories and memoirs to become familiar with it and all will help you grasp the feeling of impending radical change, coupled with frustration with the pace of change, that is present in the essays in this book.

John Holt had a particular place in the uproar of the sixties: he was among the foremost advocates for free schools, student rights, and education reform. His previous books, *How Children Fail* and *How Children Learn*, catapulted him from his job as a fifth grade private school teacher to a national speaker and consultant about how to improve schools. He was in demand as a public speaker and appeared on national media to talk about his ideas and how our schools could be changed into better places for children to learn in. While traveling around the country Holt visited hundreds of schools, speaking to both faculty and students about their experiences, noting and thinking about what he was learning.

Towards the end of *The Underachieving School* Holt notes how he would be a visiting lecturer in education at Harvard University and at the University of California/Berkeley in the next year. Holt was also an outspoken critic of the Vietnam war and an enthusiastic supporter of student organizations. It seems that he was so busy speaking, observing, and organizing during this period that he didn't have the time to write a new book. However, his writing was very much in demand and appeared in some of the most popular publications of the sixties, as well as in radical publications that Holt wanted to help gain more readers. The best of these articles were chosen by Holt for this book. The variety of places Holt's voice was heard in the sixties is impressive: *Redbook, The New York Review of Books, Life Magazine, The NY Times Magazine, The Saturday Evening Post, Book Week, The Center for the Study of Democratic Institutions, Broadside 2.* The essays cover an incredible range of issues and, in a few instances, foreshadow where Holt's thoughts would take him in the seventies when he became one of the most famous advocates for homeschooling.

John was at the top of his profession, so to speak, during the late sixties. His first two books were bestsellers and his services were in demand: *Library Journal* reviewed *The Underachieving School* and proclaimed, "This book may stir up almost as much debate as John Dewey's *Democracy and Education.*" The issues Holt wrote about then are still hot topics today and there is a "the more things change the more they stay the same" feeling that comes over you as you read this book. I think it is difficult to improve on any of Holt's critiques of testing, compulsory schooling, prestige colleges, extrinsic versus intrinsic motivations for learning, the rat race, racism, poverty, and teacher education in these brief, stinging essays. For instance:

> Here and there are schools that have been turned, against their will, into high-pressure learning factories by the demands of parents. But in large part, educators themselves are the source and cause of these pressures. Increasingly, instead of developing the intellect, character, and potential of the students in their care, they are using them for their own purposes in a contest inspired by vanity and aimed at winning money and prestige. It is only in theory, today, that educational institutions serve the student; in fact, the real job of a student at any ambitious institution is, by his performance, to enhance the reputation of that institution…
>
> The pressures we put on our young people also tend to destroy their sense of power and purpose. A friend of mine, who recently graduated with honors

from a prestigious college, said that he and other students there were given so much to read that, even if you were an exceptionally good reader and spent all your time studying, you could not do as much as half of it.

Looking at work that can never be done, young people tend to feel, like many a tired businessman, that life is a rat race. They do not feel in control of their own lives. Outside forces hurry them along with no pause for breath of thought, for purposes not their own, to an unknown end. Society does not seem to them a community that they are preparing to join and shape like the city of an ancient Greek; it is more like a remote and impersonal machine that will one day bend them to its will.

Holt had an ability to present his analyses with striking candor and reason. The essay "Making Children Hate Reading" has been reprinted many times since it first appeared. And "Teachers Talk Too Much," which originally appeared in *The PTA Magazine*, has just as much relevance today:

Most discussions [in classrooms] are pretty phony, anyway. Look through any teacher's manual. Before long you will read something like this: "Have a discussion in which you bring out the following points...." Most teachers begin a discussion with "points" in mind that they want the students to say. The students know this, so they fish for clues to find out what is wanted...

The teacher's questions get more and more pointed, until they point straight to the answer. When the teacher finally gets the answer he was after, he talks some more, to make sure all the students understand it is the "right" answer and why it is...

Holt's optimism about how schools would change appears in these essays, but what is also evident is his openness to new ideas. Unlike most school reformers, who feel we must only work to change the school system from within, Holt was thinking about other possibilities in case that didn't work. One can see the outline of his support for alternatives to school for children, not just for the alternative schools he enthuses about in *The Underachieving School*. I was most struck by the passages that show him considering keeping children out of school altogether. In "Not So Golden Rule Days" Holt claims that compulsory attendance laws are outdated and suggests

> ... that if in the opinion of a child and his parents the school is doing him no good, or indeed doing him harm, he should not be required to attend any more frequently than he wishes. There should be no burden of proof on the parents to show that they can provide facilities, companionship with other children, and all the other things the schools happen to provide. If Billy Smith hates school, and his parents feel that he is right in hating it, they are constitutionally entitled to relief. They are not obliged to demonstrate that they can give him a perfect education as against the bad one the school is giving him. It is a fundamental legal principle that if we can show that a wrong is being done, we are not compelled to say what ought to be done in its place before we are permitted to insist that it be stopped.

Indeed many of the arguments Holt made then continue to be made by school reformers today. Today's arguments are backed by even more research and data than Holt cited in 1968, yet these voices are still not taken seriously by school authorities. We now have more tests than ever for American school children, our child suicide rate is the highest in the developed world, drug and alcohol abuse among our youth is a major problem, and disaffected youths have directed their violence at schools at ever younger ages, yet we act as though these problems would all go away if only our students got better instruction and grades in reading, writing, and arithmetic. John

Holt realized that school and society, living and learning, are all of a piece and he wanted to reunite them.

Ron Miller, in his book *Free Schools, Free People: Education and Democracy After the 1960s*, writes, "Although this outburst of protest and dissent failed to bring about the 'revolution' that many envisioned, it left a complex legacy of cultural change that continues, to this day, to pose radical alternatives to the dominant economic, political, and social forces of the modern world."

Holt's response to the demise of the revolution was not to run away, but rather to run towards what he was envisioning for education. "Back to Basics" became the rallying cry for schools in the seventies and eighties, and Holt decided that school reform failed because most people simply did not support the reforms Holt and others were proposing. Holt realized most people did not want schools to change in any meaningful way and he began to seek other avenues to help remove obstacles to the child and "any gainful or useful contribution he wants to make to society." He became an outspoken advocate for children's rights and he sought, and found, other models for education besides conventional schooling. This search culminated in his book *Instead of Education: Ways to Help People do Things Better* (1976; reprinted 2004), which, in turn, led directly to Holt's full support of the homeschooling movement in 1977.

—Patrick Farenga, co-author, *Teach Your Own:
The John Holt Book of Homeschooling*

PREFACE

THE MANY EDUCATORS AND parents with whom I have talked in recent years have convinced me, by their questions and comments, that the ideas in this book are of great concern to them. The volume itself is a collection of short pieces, many of which have appeared separately in pamphlets, magazines, and books. In some I have made cuts; others I have substantially rewritten; the remainder have been included in their original version. Since this collection may be useful in different ways to many people, it seemed a good idea to make it available as quickly as possible.

Many of our schools, and many people and things in our schools, are changing rapidly. So are my ideas as well. Thus, I have here and there added a short insertion or afterword when it seemed necessary to take account of important changes, either in education or in my own thinking.

I would like to thank the Center for the Study of Democratic Institutions, Doubleday, *Harper's Magazine*, *Life*, *New York Review of Books*, *New York Times Magazine*, the *PTA Magazine*, *Redbook*, Sterling Institute, and *Yale Alumni Magazine* who first published some of these pieces and who have made it possible for me to bring them together in this book.

—John Holt
Berkeley, California

TRUE LEARNING

TRUE LEARNING—LEARNING that is permanent and useful, that leads to intelligent action and further learning—can arise only out of the experience, interests, and concerns of the learner.

Every child, without exception, has an innate and unquenchable drive to understand the world in which he lives and to gain freedom and competence in it. Whatever truly adds to his understanding, his capacity for growth and pleasure, his powers, his sense of his own freedom, dignity, and worth may be said to be true education.

Education is something a person gets for himself, not that which someone else gives or does to him.

What young people need and want to get from their education is: one, a greater understanding of the world around them; two, a greater development of themselves; three, a chance to find their work, that is, a way in which they may use their own unique tastes and talents to grapple with the real problems of the world around them and to serve the cause of humanity.

Our society asks schools to do three things for and to children: one, pass on the traditions and higher values of our own culture; two, acquaint the child with the world in which he lives; three, prepare the child for employment and, if possible, success. All of these tasks have traditionally been done by the society, the community itself. None of them is done well by schools. None of them can or ought to be done by the schools solely or exclusively. One reason the schools are in trouble is that they have been given too many functions that are not properly or exclusively theirs.

Schools should be a resource, but not the only resource, from which children, but not only children, can take what they need and want to carry on the business of their own education. Schools should be places where people go to find out the things they want to find out and develop the skills they want to develop. The child who is educating himself—and if he doesn't no one else will—should be free, like the adult, to decide when and how much and in what way he wants to make use of whatever resources the schools can offer him. There are an infinite number of roads to education; each learner should and must be free to choose, to find, to make his own.

Children want and need and deserve and should be given, as soon as they want it, a chance to be useful in society. It is an offense to humanity to deny a child, or anyone of age, who wants to do useful work the opportunity to do it. The distinction, indeed opposition, we have made between education and work is arbitrary, unreal, and unhealthy.

Unless we have faith in the child's eagerness and ability to grow and learn, we cannot help and can only harm his education.

—1968

A Little Learning

WE HEAR QUITE OFTEN these days, from prominent thinkers about education, a theory about knowing and learning. It is one, which I feel, useful and true though it may be in some details, to be fundamentally in error. Put very simply and briefly, it is this. The learning and knowing of a child goes through three stages. In the first, he knows only what he senses: the reality immediately before him is the only reality. In the second, he has collected many of his sense impressions of the world into a kind of memory bank, a mental model of the world. Because he has this model, the child is aware of the existence of many things beyond those immediately before his senses. In the third and most advanced stage of learning, the child has been able to express his understandings of the world in words and other symbols, and has also learned, or been taught, by shifting these symbols in accordance with certain logical and agreed-on rules, to predict, in many circumstances, what the real world will do.

A simple example, drawn from one of Piaget's experiments, as described by Jerome Bruner, will make this more clear.

> Take the five-year-old faced with two equal beakers, each filled to the same level with water. He will say that they are equal. Now pour the contents of one of the beakers into another that is taller and thinner and ask whether there is the same amount in both. The child will deny it, pointing out that one of them has more "because the water is higher." The child is fooled by what he sees, and because he has nothing to go on but what he sees. But when they get older,

children are no longer fooled: they say the amounts remain the same, and explain what they see with remarks like. "It looks different, but it really isn't," or "It looks higher, but that's because it's thinner," and so on.

We are told that it is because the older children can say such things, because they have learned, so to speak, to solve this problem by a verbal formula, that they are not fooled by what they see. "Language provides the means of getting free of immediate appearance as the sole basis of judgement."

Yes, it does. Or at least, it can. But it can also provide the means of saying, as men did for centuries, along with many other logically arrived-at absurdities, that since it is weight that makes bodies fall, heavier bodies must fall faster than light ones. When we try to predict reality by manipulating verbal symbols of reality, we may get truth; we are more likely to get nonsense.

Many current learning theories are closely related to those of Piaget. To see the flaw in their reasoning, we must look at one of Piaget's simpler experiments. Before a young child he put two rods of equal length, their ends lined up, and then asked the child which was longer, or whether they were the same length. The child would say that they were the same. Then Piaget moved a rod, so that their ends were no longer in line, and asked the question again. This time the child would always say that one or other of the rods was longer. From this Piaget concluded that the child thought that one rod had become longer, and hence, that children below a certain age were incapable of understanding the idea of conservation of length. But what Piaget failed to understand or imagine was that the child's understanding of the question and his own might not be the same. What does a little child understand the word "longer" to mean? It means *the one that sticks out*. Only after considerable experience does he realize that "Which is longer?" really means, "if you line them up at one end, which one sticks out past the other?" The *meaning* of the question, "Which is longer?" like the meaning of many questions, lies in the procedure you must follow to answer it; if you don't know the procedure, you don't know the meaning of the question.

Many other experiments of conservation, and other concepts as well, are flawed in the same way. A child is shown a lump of clay; then the experimenter breaks the lump into many small lumps, or stretches it into a long cylinder, or otherwise deforms it, and then asks the child whether there is more than before, or less, or the same. (When a film of this experiment was shown to a large group of psychologists and educators, nobody thought it worth mentioning that most of the time the child was looking not at the clay but at the face of his questioner, as if to read there the wanted answer—but this is another story.) The child always answered "More." The theorists say, "Aha! He says it's more because it looks like more." But to the young child the question "Is it more?" *means* "Does it look like more?" What else *could* it mean? He has not had the kind of experience that would tell him that "more" could refer to anything but immediate appearance.

I have often thought: if little children really believed about conservation what Piaget says they believe, how would their knowledge lead them to act! To make any good thing—a collection of toys, a piece of candy or cake, a glass of juice—look like more, the child would divide it, spread it about. But they don't break the candy in little bits and pour their juice into many glasses; if anything, they tend to do the opposite, gather things together into a big lump. I also asked myself, what kinds of experience might make a child aware of conservation in liquids? How would you learn that, given some liquid to drink, whatever you put it in, you got only the same amount to drink? Well, you might learn if liquid was scarce, and every swallow counted, and was counted, and relished. So I was not surprised to hear that, when someone tried the liquid conservation problem in one of the desert countries of Africa, the children caught on at a much earlier age. As they say, it figured. Finally there are some very important respects in which all children do grasp the principle of conservation, and this long before they talk well enough to learn it through words. We are told little children are fooled by their senses because they have no words to make an invariant world with. But the world they see, like the world we see, is one in which every object changes its size, shape, and position relative to other objects, every time we move. It is a world of rubber. But even by the time they are four, or three, or younger still, children know that this rubber world they see is not what the real world is like. They know that their mother doesn't shrink as she moves away from them. And this is a far more subtle understanding than the ones Piaget and others like to test.

From this fundamental error—the idea that our understanding of reality is fundamentally verbal or symbolic, and that thinking, certainly in its highest form, is the manipulation of those symbols—flow many other errors, and not just in the classroom. Having given a group of things the same label, because in a given context they have important qualities in common, we then tend to think and act as if they were permanently and in all respects identical. This often puts us badly out of touch with reality, and gets us into very serious difficulties, as in the case of our foreign policy, still largely based on the crazy notion that all Communists are alike (like Joe Stalin, to be specific), and forever the same. We think, and above all in the classroom, that almost any experience, insight, or understanding can be conveyed from one person to another by means of words. We are constantly talking and explaining, aloud or in print. But as classroom teachers know too well, our explanations confuse more than they explain, and classrooms are full of children who have become so distrustful of words, and their own ability to get meaning from words, that they will not do anything until they are shown something they can imitate.

What we must remember about words is that they are like freight cars; they may carry a cargo of meaning, of associated, nonverbal reality, or they may not. The words that enter our minds with a cargo of meaning make more complete and accurate our nonverbal model of the universe. Other words just rattle around in our heads. We may be able to spit them out, or shuffle them around according to the rules, but they have not changed what we really know and understand about things. One of the things that is so wrong with school is that most of the words children hear there carry no nonverbal meaning whatever, and so add nothing to their real understanding, instead they only confuse them, or worse yet, encourage them to feel that if they can talk glibly about something it means that they understand it. It is a dangerous delusion. As Robert Frost said, in the poem "At Woodward's Gardens," "It's knowing what to do with things that counts." No collection of theorists, however learned their theories, however precise their equations, can ever know more about the ballistics of a batted baseball than a skilled outfielder like Carl Yastremski or Willie Mays. They might have the words and figures, but he has a model that works, that tells him where that fly ball is going to come down—and that is what real knowledge is about.

One of the great OK phrases among many of the new curriculum reformers is "concept formation." Arguments rage about this. The old-fashioned say that we must teach facts, that you can't make or think about concepts unless you have a big store of facts. The reformers say we must teach concepts. The difference is not so fundamental or important as the reformers like to think. Both groups are trying to plant strings of words in children's heads. What the reformers say is that some word strings are more important than others, that there is a kind of hierarchy of ideas, with a few master ideas at the top, like the master keys that will open all the doors in a building. If you know these master ideas, then it will be easy to find out or understand anything else you want to learn. The notion is plausible and tempting. What the reformers, like most conscientious teachers, do not see is that each of us has to forge his own master key out of his own materials, has to make sense of the world in his own way, and that no two people will ever do it in the same way. If the makers of one new Social Studies curriculum have their own way, every sixth grader in the country will one day be able to say that what makes men human is that they have opposable thumbs, tools, language in which word order can influence meaning, etc. For these experts, these verbal freight cars carry an enormous load of associated meaning. For the students, they will be just a few additions to their lists of what they call "cepts"—pat phrases you put down on an exam to make a teacher think you know the course, empty of any other meaning.

The theorists and reformers do not, even yet, understand well enough what classrooms are like to children, and what really goes on there. One of the ablest and most perceptive of them, the mathematician David Page, has said that "when children give wrong answers it is not so often that they are wrong as that they are answering another question...." This is only the beginning of the truth. Sometimes children give wrong answers because they have not understood a particular question. Most of the time the trouble lies deeper. It isn't just that they do not understand the particular question, but that they don't understand the nature and purpose of questions in general. It isn't just that they now and then give an answer to a wrong problem, but that the answers they give are rarely related to any problem. A question is supposed to direct our attention to a problem; to many or most children, it does the opposite—directs their attention away from the problem, and towards the complicated strategies for finding, or stealing, an answer. But we must look further yet; for a great many of the answers children give in school they do not expect or in some cases even intend to be right. They are desperately wild guesses, or deliberately wrong ones, thrown out in the hope of evading the issue, or even of failing on purpose, to avoid the pain and humiliation of fruitless and futile effort.

If the new educational reformers do not see more clearly than they do, it is not because they have not good eyes, but for two other reasons. The first is that they tend to start talking before they have done enough looking, and their theories obstruct and blur their vision and the vision of others. The second is that their contact with schools is so special and artificial that they don't really know what school is like. On the whole, only the most successful and confident schools will even let these high-powered visitors in. Then they steer them towards their "best" classes, where a well-prepared teacher and students put on a good show. Even when the visitors do the teaching, this too is artificial. They hold no power over the students, have no rewards or penalties to hand out. The children are as glad to see a visitor come to class as to see a guest come home for dinner. For a while, they are safe. The visitor will cause them no trouble, and while he is there they are much less likely to get trouble from the usual sources. So when the reformers, who are good with children, invite them to play intellectual games, the children play freely, and therefore well. Later, the reformers go away saying "See? Anyone can do it!" not realizing that their success came, not so much from their ideas, but from their having, by being there, turned the classroom into a very different kind of place. And this, not the making of new curricula and high-powered and high-priced gadgets, is what we most need in education—to make the classroom into a very different kind of place.

—1966

Schools Are Bad Places for Kids

Of course, not all schools are alike. Some that I know of are very good. Of those that are not so good, some are much better than others, and many are getting better. Moreover, I have talked to enough school people, teachers, planners, administrators at all levels, to know that many of them are very unhappy about our schools as they are, and would like to make them much better places for kids, if they only knew how, or dared.

Still, most of our schools remain about what they have always been, bad places for children, or for that matter, anyone to be in, to live in, to learn in. In the first place, there is still a lot of cruelty in them. The story that Jonathan Kozol told about the schools of Boston could be told about almost any other big city, as many people who have grown up or taught in other cities have told me. A professor of psychology, at a college where many of the students do practice teaching in a nearby medium-sized city, told me not long ago that one of them, when she went to a school to teach, was handed a stick by the principal and told, "I don't care whether you teach them anything or not, just keep them quiet." Needless to say, the children were poor; rich parents generally don't put up with this. The incident was not unusual, but common. Many of this man's students, still hopeful and idealistic about children and education, came back from their practice teaching in tears, saying "I don't want to beat kids." But in too many schools this is still the name of the game.

I read once that in this country, and Great Britain too, the societies for the prevention of cruelty to animals have far more members and money than the societies for the prevention of cruelty to children. Interesting.

But few people in education will openly defend cruelty to children, except perhaps a few of our right-wing screwballs, so there is not much point in attacking it. Anyway, children can often resist cruelty. It is at least direct and open. When someone is hitting you with a stick, or deliberately making you feel like a fool in front of a class, you know what is being done to you and who is doing it. You know who your enemy is. But most of the harm that is done to children in schools they can't and don't resist, because they don't know what is being done to them or who is doing it, or because, if they do know, they think it is being done by kindly people for their own good.

Almost every child, on the first day he sets foot in a school building, is smarter, more curious, less afraid of what he doesn't know, better at finding and figuring things out, more confident, resourceful, persistent, and independent, than he will ever again be in his schooling or, unless he is very unusual and lucky, for the rest of his life. Already, by paying close attention to and interacting with the world and people around him, and without any school-type formal instruction, he has done a task far more difficult, complicated, and abstract than anything he will be asked to do in school or than any of his teachers has done for years. He has solved the mystery of language. He has discovered it—babies don't even know that language exists— and he has found out how it works and learned to use it. He has done it, as I described in my book *How Children Learn*, by exploring, by experimenting, by developing his own model of the grammar of language, by trying it out and seeing whether it works, by gradually changing it and refining it until it does work. And while he has been doing this, he has been learning a great many other things as well, including a great many of the "concepts" that the schools think only they can teach him, and many that are more complicated than the ones they do try to teach him.

In he comes, this curious, patient, determined, energetic, skillful learner. We sit him down at a desk, and what do we teach him? Many things. First, that learning is separate from living. "You come to school to learn," we say, as if the child hadn't been learning before, as if living were out there and learning in here and there were no connection between the two. Secondly, that he cannot be trusted to learn and is no good at it. Everything we do about reading, a task far simpler than what the child has already mastered, says to him, "If we don't make you mad, you won't, and if you don't do it exactly the way we tell you, you can't." In short, he comes to feel that learning is a passive process, something that someone else does *to* you, instead of something you do *for* yourself.

In a great many other ways he learns that he is worthless, untrustworthy, fit only to take other people's orders, a blank sheet for other people to write on. Oh, we make a lot of nice noises in school about respect for the child and individual differences and the like. But our acts, as opposed to our talk, say to the child, "Your experience, your concerns, your curiosities, your needs, what you know, what you want, what you wonder about, what you hope for, what you fear, what you like and dislike, what you are good at or not so good at—all this is of not the slightest importance, it counts for nothing. What counts here and the only thing that counts, is what we know, what we think is important, what we want you to do, think, and be." The child soon learns not to ask questions: the teacher isn't there to satisfy his curiosity. Having learned to hide his curiosity, he later learns to be ashamed of it. Given no chance to find out who he is, and to develop that person, whoever it is, he soon comes to accept the adults' evaluation of him. Like some highly advantaged eighth graders I once talked with in a high-powered private school, he thinks of himself, "I am nothing, or if something, something bad; I have no interests or concerns except trivial ones, nothing that I like is any good, for me or anyone else; any choices or decisions I make will be stupid; my only hope of surviving in this world is to cling to some authority and do what he says."

He learns many other things. He learns that to be wrong, uncertain, confused, is a crime. Right answers are what the school wants, and he learns, as I described in *How Children Fail*, countless strategies for prying these answers out of the teacher, for conning her into thinking he knows what he doesn't know. He learns to dodge, bluff, fake, cheat. He learns to be lazy. Before he came to school, he would work for hours on end, on his own, with no thought of reward, at the business of making sense of the world and gaining competence in it. In school, he learns, like every buck private or conscript laborer, to goldbrick, how not to work when the boss isn't looking, how to know when he is looking, how to make him think you are working when you know he is looking. He learns that in real life you don't do anything unless you are bribed, bullied, or conned into doing it, that nothing is worth doing for its own sake, or that if it is, you can't do it in school. He learns to be bored, to work with a small part of his mind, to escape from the reality around him into daydreams and fantasies—but not fantasies like those of his preschool years, in which he played a very active part.

There is much fine talk in schools about teaching democratic values. What the children really learn is practical slavery. How to suck up to the boss. How to keep out of trouble, and get other people in. "Teacher, Billy is...." Set into mean-spirited competition against other children, he learns that every man is the natural enemy of every other man. Life, as the strategists say, is a zero-sum game: what one wins, another must lose, for every winner there must be a loser. (Actually, our educators, above all our so-called and self-styled prestigious universities, have turned education into a game in which for every winner there are about twenty losers.) He may be allowed to work on "committees" with other children, but always for some trivial purpose. When important work is being done—important to the school—then to help anyone else, or get help is called "cheating."

He learns, not only to be hostile, but to be indifferent—like the thirty-eight people who, over a half-hour period, saw Kitty Genovese attacked and murdered without offering help or even calling for help. He comes to school curious about other people, particularly other children. The most interesting thing in the classroom—often the only interesting thing in it—is the other children. But he has to act as if these other children, all about him, only a few feet away, were not really there. He cannot interact with them, talk with them, smile at them, often even look at them. In many schools he can't talk to other children in the halls between classes; in more than a few, and some of these in stylish suburbs, he can't even talk to them at lunch. Splendid training for a world in which, when you're not studying the other person to figure out how to do him in, you pay no attention to him.

In fact, he learns how to live without paying attention to anything going on around him. You might say that school is a long lesson in

How To Turn Yourself Off, which may be one reason why so many young people, seeking the awareness of the world and responsiveness to it they had when they were little, think they can only find it in drugs. Aside from being boring, the school is almost always ugly, cold, and inhuman, even the most stylish, glass-windowed, $20-a-square-foot schools. I have by now been in a good many school buildings—hundreds, many of them very new, but I can count on the fingers of two hands those in which the halls were made more alive and human by art or decoration, of the children or anyone else—pictures, murals, sculpture. Usually, the only thing that may be legitimately put up on the walls is a sign saying "Beat Jonesville" or "Go You Vampires" or the like.

Sit still! Be quiet! These are the great watchwords of school. If an enemy spy from outer space were planning to take over earth, and if his strategy were to prepare mankind for this takeover by making men's children as stupid as possible, he could find no better way to do it than to require them, for many hours a day, to be still and quiet. It is absolutely guaranteed to work. Children live all of a piece. Their bodies, their muscles, their voices, and their brains are all hooked together. Turn off a part of them, and you turn them off altogether.

Not long ago I visited a wonderful and radical school, founded and run by young people just out of college or still in college—the Children's Community in Ann Arbor, Michigan. [This school, in the prosperous home town of one of our largest and most highly regarded universities, has had to close, temporarily and perhaps permanently, for lack of money.] That year the school had been given the use of two rooms in the Friends' Meeting House, one quite small, the other average classroom size. The children had suggested and demanded that the smaller room be set aside for quiet activities—reading, storytelling, thinking, painting, work with numbers, talking, Cuisenaire rods, puzzles, and so on, leaving the larger room free for all kinds of active and noisy work and play. Active and noisy it certainly was. About half of the children were black, and most were poor—what we now call "disadvantaged," to hide the awkward fact that what poor people lack and need is mostly money. These children spent a lot of their time playing, much more noisily and actively than even so-called "progressive" schools would allow. And as they played, they talked, to teachers and each other, loudly and excitedly, yes, but also fluently and expressively. They seemed not to have heard the news that poor kids, especially poor black kids, have no vocabulary and talk only in grunts and monosyllables.

Again, late last summer, in Santa Fe, New Mexico, I watched about a half dozen little boys, poor, of Spanish-speaking families—the disadvantaged of the Southwest—playing tackle football with a wonderful young man from the city recreation department. Thanks to miraculous tact and skill, he was able to play with them without hurting or even scaring them, but without condescending to them either. Somehow he managed to make them feel he was serious but not dangerous. The little boys, the oldest hardly eight, played with great energy and surprising skill. As they played, they kept up a running fire of chatter—fluent, pertinent, very often funny. One boy, a bit dizzy and shaken up after a hard head-on tackle, sat down at the sideline and said, "Give me two minutes time out." One of the boys on the other team, cheerfully but not very sympathetically, said, "OK. One two." And so on. Yet it is almost certain that the teachers of these boys, in their still and silent classrooms, see none of this intelligence, vivacity, and wit, and consider these children stupid and unteachable.

Children have a priority of needs. For some children, some of the time, this priority is not critical. That is, if a child can't do the thing he most wants and needs to do, there may be something else, or many other things, that he can do with almost as much pleasure and satisfaction. But at other times, and particularly if or when a child is troubled, the priority may be very critical. If he can't do the thing he most wants and needs to do, he can't do anything else; he is blocked, stopped. Turn off the number one switch and all the other switches go off. What I saw at the Children's Community, and have seen in other places since, makes me feel that many children have a strong and critical need, much stronger than I had ever suspected, for violent action, physical and vocal, and for intense personal interaction. This personal interaction need not be fighting, though in most repressed classrooms, where children are held down until they become so frantic and angry that they cannot be held down any longer, this is what it usually comes to. Perhaps the best way to suggest what else it can be is to describe some of what the children at the Children's Community and elsewhere were doing.

One of the most popular toys in the Children's Community play and noise room was a group of old and beat-up tricycles. The game of the moment, when I was there, was the skid game. A little boy would stand up on the back step of the tricycle, get going as fast as he could by pushing with his other foot, and then throw the tricycle into a violent skid, usually leaving a long black tire mark on the floor. The aim was to make the most daring skid and leave the longest mark. (These marks, by the way, had to be washed from the floor before each weekend, when the Friends themselves used the room.) One little girl, no more than five, spent at least an hour sawing into a chunk of wood. With exhausting effort, she made a rather wavy slot in it several inches deep. She was not making anything except a slot: she was just sawing, changing that piece of wood, leaving her mark on it. Other children were playing in a house made of a very heavy cardboard called Tri-Wall—a fine school material, by the way. Often some children outside would be trying to get in while others were trying to keep them out. This caused much excitement. Later a boy, or some boys, got inside another Tri-Wall box, with somewhat lower walls, and discovered that since the corners were hinged they could change its shape into a diamond. Soon they had made it into a very narrow and pointed diamond and were moving it around on the floor, pretending that it was a monster. Naturally this monster pursued other children, who fled from it, or pushed back against it. Either way, more excitement. Later some of the children and teachers got into, or fell into, a game in which the object was to hit someone else with a scarf and then run away or hide before he could hit you.

The need of poor children for this kind of play, noise, excitement, personal encounter, may be stronger than that of most children, but all children need it and love it. Some of the best children's games I have ever seen took place at the Walden Community School in Berkeley, California. This is a private elementary school, whose building costs, by the way, were cut by about one third by using the volunteer labor of parents and friends. The children there are mostly white, and mostly middle-class, not rich, but a good deal richer than most of the children at the Children's Community. The school day is wisely broken up by a number of free or recess periods, and during these periods many children of all ages rush to a big, largely unfurnished room that is used for many things, including dancing, sports, movies, school meetings, and so on. Usually the children put a rock record on the record player, turn up the volume good and loud, and begin to run and jump about.

One day they had taken from the closet a number of surplus parachutes—another good school material, not very expensive. Soon a game developed, in which the object was to throw part of the parachute over another child, or wrap or tangle it around him, and then drag and slide him over the floor to a pile of mattresses in the corner, all the while whirling the parachutes about. A kind of rotary tug of war, but disorganized, with the patterns continually changing. On another day a very different game developed. It started with a few children jumping from the top of a movable storage cabinet, about eight or nine feet high, onto a pile of mattresses on the floor. This took a good deal of courage, too much for some. Other children joined in, someone got out a parachute, and before long this was happening: the children, spaced around the edge of the parachute in a big, room-filling circle, would shout, "One, two three!" which later turned into "Uno, dos, tres!" At "three" or "tres" they would all lift up the parachute quickly into the air. The parachute would billow up, higher than their heads, and while it hung there in the air, some child would leap or even dive from the top of the storage cabinet into the middle of the parachute, and then onto the mattresses on the floor beneath. Even when they missed the mattress, as sometimes happened, the parachute held by all the children acted like a fireman's net and broke their fall. The children holding the parachute moved around each time, so that everyone got his turn to jump. Some skipped their turn with nothing said. The teachers said that, until that day, that game had never been played before. How many such games have those children invented?

Young children, of any age and background, have a great and unmet need to be touched, held, jostled, tumbled, picked up, swung about. I think again of my first visit to the Children's Community. Bill Ayers, the founder and head of the school, had brought me over from the University of Michigan, where I had given a talk. We went into the big room, Bill in his old clothes, I in my dark blue speech suit. The children paid no attention to me, but clustered around him, each with something to ask or say, all shouting, "Bill, Bill!" One little boy said, "Pick me up." Bill picked him up. More clamor: "Pick me up, pick me up!" Bill said, "I can't pick up two at once." For some reason, with no plan in mind, I said, "I can." For the first time they looked at me, now paying close attention. "No," they all said. "Yes, I can." I said. "I'll show you." Two boys approached, cautiously. I squatted down, got one in the crook of each arm, and stood up. Great excitement. They all gathered round to look and exclaim. I was an instant celebrity. Then, finding that with a boy in each arm I still had both hands free, I said, "What's more, I can pick up three at once." A louder chorus of "No-o-o!" I insisted, and a third volunteer came up. I squatted down, got a good grip with my hands, and stood up holding all three of them. Sensation! From then on, there was almost always one of the children hanging onto me, or riding on my shoulders, or trying to chin himself on my forearm, another good though (for me) tiring game.

On another occasion I was at a summer camp for poor boys, white and black, labeled "emotionally disturbed," from a nearby big city. At one point I went into a small room where one of the camp staff, a very sensitive and gifted worker with children, and three of the boys were talking into a tape recorder. They were shy and reticent and he, with great skill and tact, was teasing and encouraging them to talk. I sat on the floor near them, said nothing, but listened. None of the boys even so much as looked at me. But after a few minutes, one of them, to my surprise, shifted his position so that he was partly leaning against my knee. Shortly after, another moved around so that he was in contact with me. Neither of them spoke to me, looked at me, or acknowledged my presence in any other way. Not until after many minutes of this silent contact did they begin to exchange glances with me, and some time later to ask rather gruffly who I was. The touch came first, and if, like most teachers, I had withdrawn or even flinched from this touch, that would probably have ended the possibility of further contact.

But in most schools there is no contact, either with the real world, or real things, or real people.

In these dull, ugly, and inhuman places, where nobody ever says anything either very true or truthful, where everybody is playing a kind of role, as in a charade, where the teachers are no more free to respond openly and honestly to the students than the students are free to respond to the teachers or each other, where the air practically vibrates with suspicions and anxiety, the child learns to live in a kind of daze, saving his energies for those small parts of his life that are too trivial for the adults to bother with and thus remain his. Even the students who learn to beat the system, one might say especially those who beat it, despise it, and often despise themselves for giving in to it. It is a rare child indeed who can come through his schooling with much left of his curiosity, his independence, or his sense of his own dignity, competence, and worth.

So much for complaints. There is much more to be said—many others have said it—but this is enough. More than enough.

What do we need to do? Many things. Some are easy; we can do them right away. Some are hard, and may take some time. Take a hard one first. We should abolish compulsory school attendance. At the very least, we should modify it, perhaps by giving children every year a large number—fifty or sixty—of authorized absences. Our compulsory school attendance laws once served a humane and useful purpose. They protected children's rights to some schooling, against those adults who would otherwise have denied it to them in order to exploit their labor, in farm, shop, store, mine, or factory. Today, the laws help nobody, not the schools, not the teachers, not the children. To keep kids in school who would rather not be there costs the schools an enormous amount of time and trouble, to say nothing of what it costs to repair the damage that these angry and resentful prisoners do whenever they get the chance. Every teacher knows that any kid in class who, for whatever reason, would rather not be there, not only doesn't learn anything himself but makes learning harder for anyone else. As for protecting the children from exploitation, the chief and indeed only exploiters of children these days are the schools. Kids caught in the college rush more often than not work seventy hours or more a week, most of it on paper busywork. For many other kids, not going to college, school is just a useless time-wasting obstacle preventing them from earning needed money or doing some useful work, or even doing some true learning.

Objections: "If kids didn't have to go to school they'd all be out in the streets." No, they wouldn't. In the first place, even if schools stayed just the way they are, children would spend at least some time there because that's where they'd be likely to find friends; it's a natural meeting place for children. In the second place, schools wouldn't stay the way they are, they'd get better, because we would have to start making them what they ought to be right now—places where children would *want* to be. In the third place, those children who did not want to go to school could find, particularly if we stirred up our brains and gave them a little help, other things to do—the things many children now do during their summers and holidays.

Take something easier. We need to get kids out of the school buildings and give them a chance to learn about the world at first hand. It is a very recent idea, and a crazy one, that the way to teach our young people about the world they live in is to take them out of it and shut them up in brick boxes. It wouldn't have made a bit of sense even in a society much simpler than ours. Fortunately, some educators are beginning to realize this. In Philadelphia and Portland, Oregon, to pick only two places I have happened to hear about, plans are being drawn up for public schools that won't have any school buildings at all, that will take students out into the city and help them to use it and its people as a learning resource. Private schools in many cities are already doing the same thing. It makes sense. We need more of it.

As we help children get out into the world, to do their learning there, we can get more of the world into the schools. Apart from their parents, most children never have any close contact with adults except people whose sole business is children. No wonder they have no idea what adult life or work is like. We need to bring into the schools, and into contact with the children, a lot more people who are *not* full-time teachers. I know of a school that has started to invite in artists and craftsmen in residence. To a painter, or sculptor, or potter, or musician, or whatever, they say, "Come into our school for a few weeks (or months). Use this as your workshop. Let the kids watch you when you work, and if you feel like it, answer some of their questions, if they feel like asking any." In New York City, under the Teachers and Writers Collaborative, real writers, working writers, novelists, poets, playwrights, come into the schools, read their work, and talk to children—many of them poor—about the problems of their craft. The children eat it up. In another school I know of, every month or so, a practicing attorney, and a very successful one, from a nearby city comes in and talks to several classes about the law. Not the law as it is in books, but as he sees it and encounters it in his cases, his problems, his work. And the children love it. It is real, grownup, true, not "news" prettied up for children, not "My Weekly Reader," not "Social Studies," not lies and baloney.

Easier yet. Let children work together, help each other, learn from each other and each other's mistakes. We now know, from the experiences of many schools, rich suburban and poor city, that children are often the best teachers of other children. What is more important, we know that when a fifth or sixth grader who has been having trouble with reading starts helping a first grader, his own reading sharply improves. A number of schools, some rather tentatively and timidly, some more boldly, are beginning to use what some call Paired Learning. This means that you let children form partnerships with other children, do their work, even including their tests, together, and share whatever marks or results this work gets, just like the grown-ups in the real world. It seems to work. One teacher, teaching slow sections in which no students were very able, reported that when children were working in pairs the partnership did better work than either of the partners had done before. As we might expect. This could be a way of showing what is perhaps the hardest of all teacher's problems, getting children who have learned to protect their pride and self-esteem by the strategy of deliberate failure to give up that strategy and begin taking risks again.

Let the children learn to judge their own work. A child learning to talk does not learn by being corrected all the time; if corrected too much, he will stop talking. *He* compares, a thousand times a day, the difference between language as he uses it and as those around him use it. Bit by bit, he makes the necessary changes to make his language like other people's. In the same way, kids learning to do all the other things they learn without being taught—to walk, run, climb, whistle, ride a bike, skate, play games, jump rope—compare their own performances with what more skilled people do, and slowly make the needed changes. But in school we never give a child a chance to detect his mistakes, let alone correct them. We do it all for him. We act as if we thought that he would never notice a mistake unless it was pointed out to him, or correct it unless he was made to. Soon he becomes dependent on the expert. Let him do it himself. Let him figure out, with the help of other children if he wants it, what this word says, what is the answer to that problem, whether this is a good way of saying or doing this or not. If right answers are involved, as in some math or science, give him the answer book. Let him correct his own papers. Why should we teachers waste time on such donkey work? Our job should be to help the kid when he tells us that he can't find the way to get the right answer. Let's get rid of all this nonsense of grades, exams, marks. We don't know how, and we never will know how to measure what another person knows or understands. We certainly can't find out by asking questions. All we find out is what he doesn't know—which is what our tests are for, anyway, traps designed to catch students. Throw it all out, and let the children learn what every educated person must some day learn, how to measure his own understanding, how to know what he knows or does not know.

Some harder reforms. Abolish the fixed, required curriculum. People remember only what is interesting and useful to them, what helps make sense of the world or helps them enjoy or get along in it. All else they quickly forget, if they ever learn it at all. The idea of the "body of knowledge," to be picked up at school and used for the rest of one's life, is nonsense in a world as complicated and rapidly changing as ours. Anyway, the most important questions and problems of our time are not *in* the curriculum, not even in the hot-shot universities, let alone the schools. Check any university catalogue and see how many courses you can find on such questions as Peace, Poverty, Race, Environmental Pollution, and so on.

Children want, more than they want anything else and even after many years of miseducation, to make sense of the world, themselves, and other human beings. Let them get at this job, with our help if they ask for it, in the way that makes most sense to them. Anxious parents and teachers say, "But suppose they fail to learn something essential, something they will need to get on in the world?" Don't worry; if it is essential in the world, they will find it and learn it out there. The adults say, "Suppose they don't learn something they will need later?" The time to learn something is *when* you need it; no one can know what he will need to learn in the future; much of the knowledge we will need twenty years from now may not even exist today. The adults say, "If you let children make choices they will make bad ones." Of course, they will make some horrible ones. But how can a person learn to make good choices, except by making them, and living with them? What is more important, how can a person learn to recognize and change his bad choices, to correct mistakes, if he never has a chance to make any mistakes, or if all his mistakes are corrected for him? Most important of all, how is a child who is never given real choices to make going to think of himself as a person who is capable of making choices and decisions? If he thinks he cannot be trusted to manage his own life, to whom is he going to turn to manage it for him?

What this all boils down to is, are we trying to raise sheep— timid, docile, easily driven or led—or free men? If what we want is sheep, our schools are perfect as they are. If what we want is free men, we'd better start making some big changes.

—1969

THE FOURTH R: THE RAT RACE

MOST OF WHAT IS SAID AND written about the tremendous pressure for high grades that burdens so many young people today implies that schools and colleges are not really responsible for these pressures, that they are the innocent victims of anxious and ambitious parents on the one hand, and the inexorable demands of an increasingly complicated society on the other. There is some truth in this, but not much. Here and there are schools that have been turned, against their will, into high-pressure learning factories by the demands of parents. But in large part, educators themselves are the source and cause of these pressures. Increasingly, instead of developing the intellect, character, and potential of the students in their care, they are using them for their own purposes in a contest inspired by vanity and aimed at winning money and prestige. It is only in theory, today, that educational institutions serve the student; in fact, the real job of a student at any ambitious institution is, by his performance, to enhance the reputation of that institution.

This is true not only of colleges and universities. I have heard teachers at secondary and even elementary schools say, in reply to the just claim that students were over worried and overworked, that if students were less burdened, their test and examination scores would go down and the reputation of the school would suffer. I can still hear, in my mind's ear, the voice of a veteran teacher at a prestigious elementary school saying at a faculty meeting that if the achievement-test scores of the students did not keep pace with those of competing schools, the school would have to "close its doors"—and this in spite of the fact that it had a long waiting-list of applicants. I know of a school in which, at least for a while, the teachers' salaries were adjusted up or down according to the achievement-test scores of their classes.

Not long ago, I went to an alumni dinner of a leading New England preparatory school and there heard one of the faculty, in a speech, boast about the percentage of students who had been admitted to the college of their first choice, the number who had gone directly into the sophomore class at college, and so on. The tone was that of a manufacturer bragging that his product was better than those of his competitors. Conversely, when the faculty of a school meets to discuss the students who are not doing well in their studies, the tone is likely to be that of management considering an inferior product, one not worthy of bearing the company's name and which they are about to drop from the line. There is sometimes concern and regret that the school is not doing well enough by the child; much more often there is concern, and resentment, that the child is not doing well enough by the school.

I do not think it is in any way an exaggeration to say that many students, particularly the ablest ones, are being as mercilessly exploited by ambitious schools as they are by business and commerce, which use them as consumers and subject them to heavy and destructive psychological pressures.

In such schools, children from the age of twelve or thirteen on are very likely to have, after a long day at school, two, three or more hours of homework a night—with more over the weekend. The load grows heavier as children get older. Long before they reach college, many children are putting in a seventy-hour week—or more. Children have not worked such long hours since the early and brutal days of the Industrial Revolution.

One of my own students, a girl just turned fourteen, said not long ago, more in a spirit of wry amusement than of complaint, that she went home every night on a commuter train with businessmen, most of whom could look forward to an evening of relaxation with their families, while she had at least two or three hours' more work to do. And probably a good many of those men find their work during the day less difficult and demanding than her schoolwork is for her.

Schools and colleges claim in defense that they are compelled to put heavy pressure on students because of society's need for ever more highly trained men and women, etc., etc. The excuse is, for the most part, untrue and dishonest.

The blunt fact is that educators' chief concern is to be able to say, to college-hunting parents on the one hand, and to employee-hunting executives on the other, that their college is harder to get into, and therefore better, than other colleges, and therefore the one to which the best students should be sent and from which the best employees and graduate students can be drawn.

In a recent private talk with some of the teachers at a men's Ivy League college, I said that the job of our universities was not to provide vocational training for the future holders of top positions in business, government, science and the learned professions; it was to help boys and girls become, in the broadest sense of the word, educated adults and citizens. In return, I was asked a most revealing and interesting question: If a college does not turn out future "leaders," where in future years will it get the money for its alumni fund, the money it needs to stay in the prestige race? Where indeed? A difficult problem. But not one that should be the primary concern of educators, and certainly not one that justifies the kind of pressure for grades that is now bearing heavily on more and more children.

What are the effects of these pressures? They are many and all harmful. They create in young children an exaggerated concern with getting right answers and avoiding mistakes; they drive them into defensive strategies of learning and behavior that choke off their intellectual powers and make real learning all but impossible.

On older children, like the teenagers I now teach, the effects are even wider and more harmful. This is perhaps the time in a growing person's life when he most needs to be free of pressure. It is at this period of his life that he becomes most sharply aware of himself as a person, of the need to know who and what that person is, and of the fact that he can and will to a large extent determine who and what that person becomes. In short, it is at this time that he begins not only to know himself but also consciously to create himself, to feel intuitively what Thoreau meant when he said that every man is his own masterpiece.

A person's identity is made up of those things—qualities, tastes, beliefs—that are uniquely his, that he found and chose and took for himself, that cannot be lost or taken from him, that do not depend on his position or his success or other people's opinion of him. More specifically, it is the people he admires; the books, the music, the games, the interests that he chooses for himself and likes, whether or not anyone else likes them, or whether or not they are supposed to be "good" or "worthwhile"; the experiences that he seeks out for himself and that add to his life.

An adolescent needs time to do this kind of seeking, tasting, selecting and rejecting. He needs time to talk and think about who he is and how he got to be that way and what he would like to be and how he can get there. He needs time to taste experience and to digest it. We don't give him enough.

In addition, by putting him in a position where he is always being judged and where his whole future may depend on those judgements, we require the adolescent to direct his attention, not to who he is or ought to be or wants to be, but who we think he is and want him to be. He has to keep thinking about the impression he is making on us—his elders, the world. Thus we help to exaggerate what is already, in most young people, a serious and crippling fault—an excessive concern with what others think of them.

Since our judgements are more often than not critical, unfavorable, even harsh, we exaggerate another fault, equally serious and crippling—a tendency to imagine that other people think less well of them than in fact they do, or what is worse, that they do not deserve to be well thought of. Youth ought to be a time when people acquire a sense not just of their own identity but also of their own worth. We make it almost certain to be the very opposite.

In this competition into which we have driven children, almost everyone loses. It is not enough any more for most parents or most schools that a child should go to college and do well there. It is not even enough for most children themselves. More and more, the only acceptable goal is to get into a prestigious college; to do anything else is to fail. Thus I hear boys and girls say, "I wanted to go to so-and-so, but I'm not good enough." It is outrageous that they should think this way, that they should judge themselves stupid and worthless because of the opinion of some remote college admissions officer.

The pressures we put on our young people also tend to destroy their sense of power and purpose. A friend of mine, who recently graduated with honors from a prestigious college, said that he and other students there were given so much to read that, even if you were an exceptionally good reader and spent all your time studying, you could not do as much as half of it.

Looking at work that can never be done, young people tend to feel, like many a tired businessman, that life is a rat race. They do not feel in control of their own lives. Outside forces hurry them along with no pause for breath or thought, for purposes not their own, to an unknown end. Society does not seem to them a community that they are preparing to join and shape like the city of an ancient Greek; it is more like a remote and impersonal machine that will one day bend them to its will.

My students ask, "How can I defend myself, the real person within me, against society?" Having asked the question they gloomily decide that it cannot be done. This is, I think, what Paul Goodman meant when he said that we have imposed on the elite of our younger generation a morale fit for slaves. We have given them a sense not of mission and vocation, but of subjection and slavery. They do not seek more knowledge and power so that they may one day do great work of their own choosing: instead, they do their tasks, doggedly and often well, because they dare not refuse.

Along with their sense of mission, we destroy to a very considerable extent their sense of joy, both in work and in leisure. Thoreau once wrote: "The truly efficient laborer will not crowd his day with work, but saunter to the task surrounded by a wide halo of ease and leisure." The man is badly cheated who has never felt that he could not wait to get back to his work and, so feeling, hurled himself into it with fierce joy. Not only is he cheated; the work he does is probably neither well done nor much worth doing.

I think of a student of mine, years ago, kept on campus week-end after week-end, for not having his work done—presumably so that he could use the time to get it done. On one such week-end, I found him working on one of his hobbies, a small printing press. In exasperation I said to him, "If you'd just do the things you have to do and get them out of the way, then you could be free to do the things you want to do."

With tired wisdom, much greater than mine, he said, mildly: "No, you can't. They just give you more things you have to do."

It is truer now than it was then. Schools cannot bring themselves to say, "That's enough." No matter how high they raise the hoop, if a child manages to jump through it, they take his success as a signal that they must raise it still higher.

The gross effects of these pressures are painfully evident. Along with an increase in psychological disturbances, we have increases in suicide, in the use or overuse of alcohol, and in drug-taking. We also read of a great increase in all kinds of cheating, not among unsuccessful students, but among superior students whose grades would be very good even if they did not cheat. It is no small thing that large numbers of our young people, supposedly our ablest and best, are becoming convinced that they must cheat in order to succeed; that success is so important that it justifies the cheating.

But the broader and more general consequence of the pressure for grades is that it has debased and corrupted the act of learning itself. Not by what we say but by what we do, by the way we hand out rewards and prizes, we convince many young people that it is not for the joy and satisfaction of understanding that we learn but in order to get something for ourselves; that what counts in school and college is not knowing and understanding, but making someone think you know and understand; that knowledge is valuable, not because it helps us deal better with the problems of private and public life, but because it has become a commodity that can be sold for fancy prices on the market. School has become a kind of racket, and success in school, and hence in life, depends on learning how to beat it.

Can schools and colleges be persuaded to do away with, or greatly reduce, their demands for high grades? There are many reasons for thinking they cannot.

First, they do not seem aware of the harm that their competition for prestige is doing to American youth and American education. In fact, they take quite an opposite view, talking about higher standards and upgrading education.

Second, they would say that they have found from experience that it is the students with high test scores who have the best chance of staying in college. But this is because so much of their teaching is based on getting high test scores; if they reduced the importance of exams and marks, they would reduce the need for getting only those students who were good at taking exams.

Third, the colleges would say that unless they make entrance difficult by demanding high test scores, they will have too many applicants to choose from. But they have too many as it is, and must ultimately make many choices on the basis of criteria other than test scores. Why not make these criteria more important, and if they still have too many applicants, choose from them by lot? Under such a system, a student applying to a popular college would know that his chances of being admitted were slight, but would feel, if he was not admitted, that it was chance that had kept him out—not that he was no good.

Perhaps a number of prestigious colleges could be persuaded to agree to say jointly that they would admit some fixed percentage of applicants each year, despite low test scores, if the applicants had other important qualifications. If they found, as I believe they would, that such students were on the whole as useful and valuable as students getting very high scores, they could raise the percentage. Such a policy would encourage primary and secondary schools and teachers to work for goals other than high test scores, and it would give hope to at least a number of very talented young people who are not good at taking exams.

But if the colleges cannot be persuaded to give up, or moderate, their competition for prestige and for high-scoring students who will enhance that prestige, then the schools should resist them. A good place to begin would be by attacking the notion that only at a prestigious institution can one get a good education.

I have known, and know, students at prestigious colleges who are not interested in their courses and for whom college has not been an exciting or stimulating experience. I know other bright and able boys and girls who have been, and are being, very much excited and stimulated at institutions that have much less prestige, or none at all.

In some cases a nonprestigious institution may have fewer first-rate scholars or teachers, but it is probably true that such as there are have more time for and interest in their really able and curious students. And the students, themselves under less pressure, have more time for them.

Most important of all, the schools and their teachers must do all they can, by word and deed, to destroy the notion that education is a race against other students to win the favor of someone in authority. They must put in its place the idea that what is important—and here I use the words of the late President Griswold of Yale—is "the desire and the capacity of the individual for self-education: that is, for finding meaning, truth and enjoyment in everything he does."

There are encouraging signs that some of our leading colleges and universities are beginning to realize that grades and exam scores are not the best or the only criteria for judging applicants for admission. One of my students at the Harvard Graduate School of Education, himself a professor in an Ivy League university, told me that one of his students, who never finished sophomore year in high school but instead traveled and worked and studied independently, was later admitted to both Harvard and Brown.

Our schools have let themselves think that all the bargaining power lies with the colleges. But this is not so. Our prestigious colleges need good students as much as the students need the colleges. Suppose more and more schools began saying to colleges, "Our best students are fed up with grinding for grades: they want to learn for the interest and joy of learning. Unless you show them, and us, that you are making grades less important, they are going to look for other colleges to go to, and we are going to help them." Might this not change the picture? After all, pressure can be exerted both ways.

Taking a longer view, I cannot see why any college should not admit anyone and everyone who applied for admission. What if they get filled up? Then let them do what any theatre or movie house or concert or lecture hall does—hang out a sign that there is no more room, and that people will have to wait for the next performance. If someone wants so badly to go to Hotshot U. that he will wait four years to get in, they would be wise to let him wait in line until there is room. Most students will quite sensibly go to other places nearly as good where the line is not as long. Let overcrowding be the students' problem, not the institution's. In the same way, let a student judge whether or not he will be able to do the work at a college. If I go to a concert hall to hear a difficult piece of music, nobody gives me an exam at the door to make sure that I am going to be able to understand it. It may in fact be too difficult and I may not understand or like it, and so waste my time and money. That is my risk and my misfortune. The same is true when I buy a book, or go to a play, or a lecture, or a museum. Let the student take the same risk.

—1966

Teachers Talk Too Much

Do teachers talk too much? I'm afraid we do. Much too much. From the time we enter the school in the morning till we leave it at night, we hardly stop talking. We only realize how much we talk when we come to school with a sore throat.

What do we talk about? Some of the time we hand out information. Perhaps we read something from a text. Or we tell students something we think they ought to know—certain rules of grammar, facts about a place or an event, what a poem means, why this book is important, and so on. We like handing out information. It's our pleasure as well as our business.

Other times we demonstrate, or explain, or criticize, or correct: This is how you do long division. This is how you factor quadratic equations. This is how you do this experiment. This is how you are to write your book report. This is why you got that problem wrong. This is what you should be doing with that picture. The last may seem surprising but in my limited experience with them I have not found that art teachers are noticeably more silent than others.

Dominant in Discussion

Sometimes we run what we like to call discussions: even then, we usually talk as much as all the students put together. Not long ago I saw a videotape of an expert teacher running a discussion in social studies. His high school class talked freely, but he out-talked them. However much they managed to say, answering his questions, he managed to say more in commenting on their answers and setting up his next question.

Most discussions are pretty phony, anyway. Look through almost any teacher's manual. Before long you will read something like this: "Have a discussion in which you bring out the following points...." Most teachers begin a discussion with "points" in mind that they want the student to say. The students know this, so they fish for clues to find out what is wanted. They say, "I don't get it." "Would you please repeat the question?" "I don't quite know what you mean by...."

The teacher's questions get more and more pointed, until they point straight to the answer. When the teacher finally gets the answer he was after, he talks some more to make sure all the students understand it is the "right" answer, and why it is.

Once I was teaching a fifth grade math class and was very much pleased with myself because, instead of "telling" or "showing" a youngster, I was "making her think" by asking questions. But she didn't answer. I followed each question with another that was easier and more pointed. Still no answer. I looked hard at my silent student and discovered she didn't even looked puzzled. Just patient. Then it dawned on me: She was just waiting for that really pointed question—the one that would give her the right answer.

So-called discussion often goes that way. Students know that teachers have answers in mind. They know, too, that if they patiently persist in fishing for clues, most teachers will rise to the bait.

Much of teachers' talk, maybe most of it, is just classroom management—keeping the kids in line. Somewhere we got the crazy notion that a class would learn most efficiently if everyone was learning the same thing at the same time. As if a class were a factory.

So we have these flocks of school children, twenty-five or more of them, that we are trying to lead or drive down a chosen road. They don't all want to go down that road; maybe none of them do; they have other things they would rather do or think about. So we continually have to round them up and move them along, like a sheepdog herding sheep. Only, our voice is the dog.

"Now, children, take out paper and pencil, and turn to page thirty-four in your book. We're going to work on—Tommy, where is your pencil? What? Well, why don't you? I've told you enough times you should come to class ready for work. Everyone else is waiting for you. Come up here and I'll give you another.

"Mary, stop whispering to Helen. Is your book open to the proper page? Well, you would have heard me if you hadn't been so busy talking to each other."

And so on. We talk to get children ready to do what they are supposed to do, and then we talk to make sure they are doing it. We ask about yesterday's homework or tell about tomorrow's. We talk to keep everyone's attention focused on the front of the room.

Not long ago I saw an expert teacher, who had good rapport with his class, using a slide-film projector to do an arithmetic lesson. I began to wonder how many of the words he was speaking had to do with the actual work and how many had to do with sheepdogging—keeping the class together. It was clear after a while that there was much more sheepdogging than work—two or three times as much. This is not unusual.

Tuning Out

One result of too much teacher talk is that children who, when they were little, were turned on full all the time, learn to turn themselves off or at least down. They listen with only a small part of their being, like any adult listening to boring talk. If this goes on long enough, they forget how to turn themselves up, to listen with all their attention. They lose the knack of it, and the taste for it. It is a great loss.

Teachers think they know that children tune them out. I once watched an experienced teacher showing how some problems should be worked. His way of keeping students' attention was to call on a student and ask, "Is this right?" as he finished putting each step of a problem on the blackboard. The student who was called on would answer, "Yes," and then the teacher would go on to the next step. It was all very dull, and my mind was wandering off to other things when suddenly my attention was jerked back to the classroom.

The boy who had been asked if the answer was right was saying, "No, sir, it isn't. It ought to be so-and-so." The teacher agreed, made the change, and went on as before. Talking after class, the teacher said to me, "You notice that I threw them a little curve ball there. I do that every now and then. Keeps them on their toes." What the teacher hadn't noticed was that when he threw his curve ball his voice changed, so that the children had a signal that it was time to turn up and tune in.

Yes, teachers know that children turn them off, and they have their little tricks to try to keep the children tuned in. But the children learn the little tricks that various teachers use, and low-powered listening becomes a substitute for high-powered attention. This is too bad.

But more important is the fact that while teachers talk all they want, the children get hardly any chance to talk at all. In most schools the rule is still that children may speak only when called upon by the teacher. Many schools prohibit talking between classes, more than a few prohibit talking at lunch, and I have even heard of some where children were not allowed to talk during recess.

Some will say, "What's wrong with that? Children come to school to learn, not to talk." As if learning were a passive process, like a kettle being filled at a faucet.

The trouble is that when we treat children this way, we make them bad learners. For real learning takes place only when the learner plays a dual role, when he is both learner and teacher, doer and critic, listener and speaker. The student who tries only to remember what is in his book will not even succeed in doing that. The skillful learner talks to, even argues with, the book. He asks himself questions and checks his understanding as he goes along. A poor student never knows what parts of a lesson he understands and what he does not. He leaves it to the teacher to find out.

Even in learning a skill—painting, or music, or a sport—the learner, as he performs, must continually judge his own performance, be aware of his mistakes. Am I in tune and in rhythm? Am I watching the ball? Little children learning to walk, talk, and do a hundred other things are good at this. Too often, it is school and nonstop talking teachers that turn them into inert and passive learners.

—1967

THE TYRANNY OF TESTING

LET ME NOT MINCE WORDS. Almost all educators feel that testing is a necessary part of education. I wholly disagree—I do not think that testing is necessary, or useful, or even excusable. At best, testing does more harm than good; at worst, it hinders, distorts, and corrupts the learning process. Testers say that testing techniques are being continually improved and can eventually be perfected. Maybe so—but no imaginable improvement in testing would overcome my objections to it. Our chief concern should not be to improve testing, but to find ways to eliminate it.

In some circumstances, of course, tests are necessary. If a man wants to play the violin in a symphony orchestra, it makes sense to ask him to show that he meets the orchestra's standards. If he wants to work with people who speak no English, he ought to prove that he can speak their language. If he wants a license to design and build buildings, he should show that he knows enough to keep his structures from falling down. If he wants to be a surgeon, he should prove to competent judges—on the operating table, not a piece of paper— that he can operate on people without killing them.

Very similar to these are the tests people give themselves to check their own progress. The typist types exercises to increase her rate per minute. The musician plays scales and studies, and plays difficult passages against a metronome. The tennis player serves dozens of balls, trying to place them accurately in this or that corner. The heart surgeon operates on frogs, training his fingers to work with small vessels in cramped spaces. The skater does school figures, the quarterback passes to his ends, and the pitcher throws again and again to his catcher. The pilot makes approach after approach. The student, if he is wise, puts important information on file cards—one of the most flexible, most effective, and cheapest of all teaching machines—and runs through the pack, taking the questions in many different orders. In short, all serious practice can be seen as a way in which the learner tests his own skill and knowledge.

But virtually *none* of the testing done in schools is of this kind.

Students are not, as a rule, tested to prove they can perform activities they have chosen for themselves, without endangering other people or ruining a collective enterprise. Testing in schools is done for very different reasons, and, by and large, we are not very honest about these reasons. To the public—and to ourselves—we teachers say that we test children to find out what they have learned, so that we can better know how to help them to learn more. This is about 95 percent untrue. There are two main reasons why we test children: the first is to threaten them into doing what we want done, and the second is to give us a basis for handing out the rewards and penalties on which the educational system—like all coercive systems—must operate. The threat of a test makes students do their assignment; the outcome of the test enables us to reward those who seem to do it best. The economy of the school, like that of most societies, operates on greed and fear. Tests arouse the fear and satisfy the greed.

This system may be necessary, or at least unavoidable. We may just possibly be right—though I doubt it—to feel that it is our duty to decide what children should be made to learn. And we may just possibly be right—though again I don't think so—in thinking that the best way to make children learn what we have decided they should learn is to reward or penalize them in proportion to their success or failure at learning it. But, in any case, this is nearly always what tests in school are for and we are deeply dishonest if we pretend that they are for anything else.

Many teachers, and even students, say and sincerely believe that even if tests do threaten students into working, they can be an accurate measure of the quality of their work. To me, it seems clear that the greater the threat posed by a test, the less it can measure, far less encourage, learning. There are many reasons for this. One of the most obvious, and most important, is that whenever a student knows he is being judged by the results of tests, he turns his attention from the material to the tester. What is paramount is not the course or its meaning to the student, but whatever is in the tester's mind. Learning becomes less a search than a battle of wits. The tester, whoever he is, is no longer a guide and helper, but an enemy.

Browsing through a bookstore one day several years ago, I came upon an exhaustive sociological study of medical school students. I began to read parts of it, perhaps to find out whether medical students were hindered by the same fears and self-protective and evasive strategies that so hampered my fifth graders. I soon found that they were. The authors had interviewed a great many students, at different stages in their medical education. Over and over again, these young men said that they had entered medical school passionately eager to learn medicine, only to find themselves continually being checked up on, examined, and tested and to learn that their future careers depended almost entirely on how well they did on these tests. Soon, preparing for exams came to replace learning medicine as the fundamental business of medical school. Before long, they came to judge and label their professors, not by skill or knowledge, but according to their "fairness," a fair professor being one whose tests were predictable and could thus be studied for.

The feeling that a test is a trap and the tester an adversary I have often felt myself—and even in situations in which the tester has had no power over me. One of my present students likes to cut test-yourself quizzes out of newspapers and magazines, and once in a while he bustles up to me in the halls at school, waving a piece of paper and challenging, "Let's see how smart you are!" or "Let's see how good a driver you are !" or something like that. Instantly, I feel under attack. Someone is trying to make a fool of me. If the student actually asks me some of the questions on the quiz, and I rarely let him get that far, I find myself thinking, "What's the catch? What's this guy after? How does his mind work?" I am in a duel as intense and personal as a game of chess.

If a test is a duel with an enemy who is out to do you in, any and all means of outwitting him are legitimate. This attitude is at the root of most of the cheating that has become so prevalent lately, above all among successful students in "good" schools. The line is not easy to draw between reading a teacher's mind, or making him think you know what you don't know, and outright cheating. In any case, it is not a distinction that many students under pressure are very worried about—or many teachers either. If a teacher is being judged by his students' performances on a standardized test, he joins forces with the children to outwit the common enemy by whatever means he can. A great many teachers and schools are utterly unscrupulous about this. I have taught fifth graders who, though their achievement test scores from previous years showed that they had adequate skill in arithmetic, were unable to add or subtract. How, then, had these achievement test scores been obtained? By diligent cramming on the part of the teachers. I have at times on occasion been told to do some of this cramming myself. "Never mind what you think the children understand or can use or remember. Just see to it that they get decent marks on those achievement tests." Yet isn't this a kind of cheating?

Must a test be a trap? When it determines who gets the carrot and who gets the stick, it cannot help but be. Churchill once said, in words more eloquent than these, that his teachers at Harrow were not interested in finding out what he knew, but only in discovering what he didn't know. This is generally true, not because teachers are old meanies, but because the system—the need to continually separate sheep from goats—demands it. Consider the problem of the test-giver. A student who knows anything at all about a subject knows enough to write about it for hours. I, for example, have not studied American history since the eighth grade and quickly forgot most of what I learned then. What little I know or think I know about it, I have picked up from a lot of miscellaneous reading, hardly any of it in what could be called history books. Yet if I were asked to write out all I know and understand about American history, it would take many pages—perhaps a book, perhaps several. How, then, can anyone test my knowledge, let alone the knowledge of a student of history, in an hour or three hours? He can't. If a teacher gives his students a test that allows them to show how much they know, they will all run out of time long before they have run out of things to say, and he will have no way to mark them except to give them all the same mark, which his bosses will not like. To make distinctions between students, which in most schools is a teacher's duty—*everyone* can't go to Harvard—he must ask questions that some students, at least, will not be able to answer. In short, like Churchill's teachers, he must seek out ignorance so that he can "objectively" decide who gets the rewards and who gets the penalties.

I have still more objections to tests. They almost always penalize the student who works slowly. Tests tend to favor the clever guesser, the player of percentages, and to put at a disadvantage the student who likes to be thorough and sure. They severely penalize the anxious students who worry about tests; because of their fears, many students are wholly unable to show on tests just how much they do know, and every failed test makes them more fearful of the next. And tests are misleading, indeed worthless, with those students—in our cities, I suspect, there are many—who make no effort to do well on them, pursuing the strategy of deliberate failure, perhaps to save face, perhaps to hurt their parents, perhaps to fight back at a system they despise.

It may be when tests seem to work best that they do the most harm. I have had frequent discussions with my present students—able, successful, on their way to prestigious colleges—about testing and grading. It is surprising how fiercely many of them defend a system that they often complain about and rebel against. They say, angrily or anxiously, "But if we're not tested and graded, how can we tell whether we're learning anything, whether we're doing well or poorly?" It makes me sad. I think of the two- and three-year-olds I have known, continually comparing their own talk to the talk of people around them. I think of the five- and six-year-olds I have known, teaching themselves to read, figuring out each new word on a page, continually checking what they are doing against what they have done, what they don't know against what they know. Then I think of my fifth graders, handing me arithmetic papers and asking anxiously, "Is it right?", and looking at me as if I were crazy when I said, "What do you think?" What difference did it make what they thought? Rightness has nothing to do with reality, or consistency, or common sense; Right is what the teacher says is Right, and the only way to find out if something is Right is to ask a teacher. Perhaps the greatest of all the wrongs we do children in school is to deprive them of the chance to judge the worth of their own work and thus destroy in them the power to make such judgements, or even the belief that they can.

What I have said so far pertains to tests within a compulsory system. But I have other, more deeply rooted objections to testing, even in a system which uses no threats or coercion whatever. These objections rest on beliefs about the nature of thought, knowledge, learning, and education. Perhaps the following story will shed light on some of them.

Many years ago I worked in the movement promoting the idea of world government. One day I met an old and close friend whom I had not seen for some time. He asked me what I was doing, and when I told him, he began to argue with me. I was wasting my time, he said, and doing harm. His argument was a familiar one: that by talking about the need for world government we were undermining confidence in the United Nations and contributing to its destruction. By that time, I had learned not to argue with close friends, but to try instead to find out why they thought as they did. I encouraged him to go on talking. Slowly, in the course of a talk over lunch, his deeper feeling about the world began to emerge. By the end of lunch, he was saying that China was our great enemy and that we should conquer her while we had a monopoly on atomic weapons. As for the United Nations, the least that could be said against it was that it was a nuisance and an impediment. At worst, it was a positive danger, and the sooner we were out of it, the better.

In the space of less than two hours, my friend had expressed concern that I was undermining the United Nations and then denounced it as worthless and dangerous. To hear one person state such diametrically opposed views, not only sincerely but passionately, was a great shock to me. In time, I came to learn that this was not in the least unusual. It is common to hear even supposedly intelligent and informed people make statements, often within a short space of time, that flatly contradict each other. The makers of polls know that it is possible to get widely differing answers to a given question by varying the phrasing of the question, or the context of questions leading up to it. Polls on the Vietnam War show, time after time, that many people hold conflicting and contradictory beliefs. Only a few years ago, it seemed clear that the large majority of white Americans genuinely approved and supported blacks' desires and demands for equality. Events have since shown that many, perhaps most, of these people are strongly opposed to any such progress if it in any way affects their own lives. Yet they were not lying before; they simply did not know what they would do in a pinch.

Few of us do. And this is my chief and fundamental reason for doubting the value of testing. How can we expect to measure the contents of someone else's mind when it is so difficult, so nearly impossible, to know more than a very small part of the contents of our own? Human psychology—the psychology of thought and feeling, not perception—is still an infant science. Those who practice it disagree about a great many things. But there is one matter about which they do seem to agree—that about a great many important things we quite literally do not know what we think. To learn even a part of the contents of our own minds is a most slow, subtle, difficult, often painful task. How then, I must ask again, can we be so sure of our ability to discover the contents of the minds of others?

The argument can be made, of course, that though it is difficult or even impossible to find out how someone feels about, say, his own father, it is not necessarily difficult to find out what he thinks about geometry, Shakespeare, or electrical engineering. There is some truth in this. Most men are more likely to know what they really think about income taxes than what they really think about their families, and what they say about income taxes may be fairly close to their real thoughts. But only fairly close, and only some of the time. We carry about in our minds many strings of words—rules, maxims, principles—which we have learned are appropriate and comfortable on certain occasions, but which have little or nothing to do with what we really believe or with the way we really conduct our lives. In short, even on homely, mundane matters, what we say, and sincerely say, may be far removed from what we really think.

Even if our society comes to value knowledge of self more than knowledge of space, and all men become philosophers, which is in part the proper business of us all, even if we know what we ourselves think, there will remain reasons why it will be difficult to know what other people, and particularly children, think. The following excerpts from an unpublished paper by Tony Kallet, one of the School Advisors in Leicestershire, England, may shed some light on them:

Some Thoughts on Applied Piaget

Here is a transcript of a small part of a film suggesting ways in which teachers can use some of Piaget's experimental tasks as means of finding out about children's mathematical progress in the classroom. The film is part of a series entitled "Children and Mathematics" prepared by the Nuffield Mathematics project and presented on the BBC. The scene I have transcribed shows an adult (not, I think, the child's regular teacher) and a boy of perhaps six or seven who has on the table in front of him three tulips and six or seven daisies.

> ADULT: Are there more flowers or more daisies?
> CHILD: More daisies.
> A: More daisies. Right. Now, I'm just wondering whether there aren't more flowers, because the daisies are part of the flowers, that's right, isn't it?
> C: Yes.
> A: And the tulips are also part of the flowers?
> C: (Does not reply)
> A: Is that right?
> C: Yes.
> A: And so the whole lot of them are flowers. Now, I think they are all flowers but only these ones (pointing) are daisies. So I think there are more flowers than daisies.
> C: (Does not reply)
> A: Now, does that make sense?
> C: (After a long pause) No.
> A: (With a chuckle) Are there more flowers or more daisies?
> C: More daisies.
> A: More daisies.
> COMMENTATOR: Who would imagine that this is the child's view of the world.

Who indeed?

Let me also say, however, that an experimental situation such as the one portrayed here does not, in my opinion, shed light on the child's thinking about part-whole relationships nearly so much as it sheds light on his willingness, or, in this case, unwillingness, to engage in a type of classroom dialogue with an adult the rules of which are known to both—the child's job is to figure out what the adult expects him to say, and the adult's job is to make this as easy as possible for the child....

On the evidence supplied, then, I think we cannot infer anything about this boy's understanding of part-whole relationships. It is quite possible that his understanding is poor, but I am quite confident that in *meaningful* [italics mine] situations in which part-whole relationships had to he dealt with operationally, he would show more comprehension than in this abstract verbal sparring in which he is scarcely free at all to think about the things in front of him.

Mr. Kallet's comments are more generous and temperate than mine would be. I find this adult-child interview outrageous, almost sinister. I find it even more outrageous that it should have been widely disseminated as an example of the latest thing in psychological research and that it was received as such without a storm of protest.

Mr. Kallet continues:

I have found it revealing over the past few years to enquire of children and adults whether there are, or were, more children or more people in their families. The following is a representative dialogue:

ME: How many children are there in your family?
CHILD: Three.
M: How many grown-ups?
C: Two.
M: Are children people?

C: Yes. (Although some children, even of nine or
ten, need to stop and ponder this.)

M: Now, are there more children in your family or
more people?

C: More children.

Alternative answers have been on the following
lines: (1) Huh? You can't ask that; (2) More children
naturally; (3) Huh? what do you mean? I think I can
say accurately that out of perhaps twenty children
I've asked this question of, not more than one or two
under the age of ten have given the correct answer to
my questions. In addition, I have received the same
answer from several intelligent adults. Note that if
my question had been "Are there more children or
more adults?" the answer would have been correct.

When I first read about Piaget's part-whole experiments, it
seemed likely to me that, regardless of what they had been told, the
children were in fact comparing one part of the class (of beads or
flowers or whatever) to the part that was left. This was the kind of
comparison they were used to making, and indeed the only one that
seemed to make any sense. A few experiments with children confirmed this: they always said that there were more of whichever of the
two subjects was larger. That some adults give the "wrong" answer to
Mr. Kallet's question strongly suggests that they see the question the
same way. It seems to me, furthermore, that if a child did at first
understand the daisy-flower or children-people question in the way
intended, he would soon dismiss it as being too silly. In plain fact, it
is silly. If someone suddenly asked me if there were more males or
people in my family, I would probably answer (1) Say that again,
please. (2) Are you kidding? (3) What do you mean? I certainly
wouldn't expect that the questioner wanted me to take such a silly
question literally and seriously.

Let me suggest an alternative experiment. Suppose we take two
photos, one of all the children in a family, the other of *all* the members of the family, adults and children. Suppose we then ask the children which photo has more people in it. Does anyone believe that any

child older than, say, four will give the wrong answer? What, then, becomes of this great confusion about parts and wholes? I suspect it proves to be largely verbal, caused by nothing more than the fact that children do not understand certain kinds of word-chains to mean what we intend them to mean.

Thus, even if we all, including little children, knew our own thoughts, the testing situation would have two grave defects irremediably built into it. The first stems from the limitations of language. The tester can never, even if he wants to, and he may not always want to, fully express, in the words of his question, what it is that he wants to find out, while the answerer cannot wholly express in his answer what he wants to reply. The second defect arises from the fact that in almost any questioning situation there is an element of judgement, and hence of threat, which must influence the thoughts and words of the two parties. The questioner, depending on what he wants, cannot help to some degree pushing the responder either towards or away from the correct answer. The responder, in turn, cannot help wondering what the tester wants and, again depending on the situation, deciding whether or not to give it to him. There is no escape from this. If someone asks me a question, one of the first thoughts that must pop into my head, is, "Why is he asking me this?" What I do from then on may depend very heavily on what I think he is after. The poignant conversation between Heyst and Lena in Joseph Conrad's novel *Victory* shows how confusions and doubts about the purposes and implications of even a loved one's words can put a stop to talk altogether, an experience that is probably painfully familiar to all of us.

I am reminded of a second grader I once knew, a bright, troubled, rebellious boy, furiously angry with his parents for reasons I didn't know. I was trying, against his will and therefore unsuccessfully, to teach him to read. One day our school psychologist, a sensitive and sensible woman, gave him a Stanford-Binet intelligence test. Not long afterward we were discussing the boy. She said, "You know something interesting about his Binet? He got many more questions right at the highest level of the test than he did at the easier levels." After more thought and talk, we tentatively decided that this boy was probably afraid to give obvious answers to easy questions, for fear that the testers might be playing a trick on him. I have had the same feeling myself, thinking of some seemingly simple question, "It can't be this easy or they wouldn't have asked it." Let me return once more to Mr. Kallet:

> Joan Tamburini, of the Froebel Institute, told me last year of a student of hers who was replicating one of Piaget's classification experiments. In this, the child is given a number of miniature representations of cars, people, dishes, silverware, etc., and is asked to put together those which he feels belong together. Young children invariably classify according to some seemingly chance or superficial schema: perhaps they put the car with the plate because they had a picnic in the country, etc. Tamburini's student, however, finished by asking the children if they would put the various pieces back in a box. And this time they quite easily and naturally grouped them in a systematic way, the vehicles together, the eating utensils together, etc. What is one to conclude about their ability to group? Surely the conclusion is that when presented with things to play with, they will play, and their play will follow its own rules, but when asked to tidy up, they will follow a more adult, "logical" convention for sorting. Do they or don't they have the concept of putting likes with dislikes of grouping according to function? Well, it all depends, it would seem, on what task they think has been set for them.

Exactly. And this is the final and inevitable problem of the tester. There is a certain response he wants to get. How shall he ask for it? What shall he say? If he makes his question too clear, he gives his answer away with the question. My fifth graders, like most children, were expert at getting teachers to ask too clear, self-answering questions. If the teacher does not make his question clear enough, it may be misunderstood. What is worse, he may not recognize that it has been misunderstood and, like many educators and psychologists, may be led by the wrong answers he gets to highly dubious conclusions.

Let me repeat. Unless we become telepathic, we can never know more than a small part—and that only approximately—of what is in the mind of another human being. Why need it trouble us so? There is no reason, except to relieve our own anxieties and insecurity, that we should constantly know what children are learning, or even why they are learning. What true education requires of us instead is faith and courage—faith that children want to make sense out of life and will work hard at it, courage to let them do it without continually poking, prying, prodding, and meddling. Is this so difficult?

—1968

NOT SO GOLDEN RULE DAYS

OUR COMPULSORY SCHOOL attendance laws stand in the way of good education. They should be relaxed, amended, repealed, or overturned in the courts.

I once felt this was necessary in the interests of children. I now have come to feel equally strongly that it is also in the best interests of the schools. It is time for our schools to get themselves, or us to get them, out of the jail business. No one can doubt that this is where they are. The public has, in effect, said to our schools, "Lock up our children for six or more hours a day for a hundred and eight or so days a year, so that they will be out of our hair and out of trouble—and, by the way, while you have them locked up, try to educate them." The two demands are contradictory and self-canceling. The schools can be in the jail business or in the education business, but not in both. To the extent that they are in the one they cannot be in the other.

There are many reasons why it would benefit our schools to get out of the jail business. One of these has to do with money. I have heard the assistant superintendent of schools in Baltimore, Maryland, describe the millions of dollars his system has to spend every year to repair broken windows and other kinds of vandalism. Who broke those windows? Who did the damage? Kids who hated being in school and therefore hated the school they were in. Vandalism by students is an act of revenge. Do away with the cause for hatred and the need for revenge, and the vandalism will stop. Teenage youths rarely throw stones through the windows of banks, hotels, drugstores. It is the schools they hate: it is the schools they try to destroy. Not long ago I heard a very intelligent and articulate young man in one of our major cities suggest, quite seriously, and altogether apart from any other kind of rioting, that all the schools in his community should be burned down at once.

There is no way of estimating how much time, effort, and money the schools spend trying to find ways to take care of the many youngsters who do not want to be there. Countless special schools, special classes, special personnel, special disciplinary regulations, special therapeutic guidance programmes, etc.—all exist almost solely to handle the problem of the child who hates being in school. It is also impossible to assess how much of the time and energy of teachers is taken up with the problem of controlling unruly prisoners.

The jail business is expensive in still another way. Since the schools have been given the job of keeping all our children in prison for a certain number of hours each day, it follows that they must see that all the prisoners are in fact there, and if they are not there, know why not, and where they are instead. This is a major source of the inordinate amount of paper work that plagues administrators and teachers alike. All the complicated attendance records that schools keep have one main purpose—to prove that all the prisoners were there or that they had a lawful excuse to be absent. If we overturn the compulsory attendance laws, this will not be needed.

I see a great many students, of all backgrounds, in the Boston Public Library. They behave as reasonably, sensibly, and considerately as anyone else. Nobody has ever hinted that their behavior might be a problem. Why not? For one thing, when you are in a place because you want to be there, you tend to behave in an appropriate way. In the second place, the students know that if they raise hell in the library they will not be allowed to return. Nothing else need be said. The kind of monitors, spies, corridor-watchers, and so on who infest our schools—to say nothing of armed, uniformed police—are not found in libraries, even in the toughest parts of our cities. There is no need for them. If the school becomes a resource to be used by the people who want it, there will be no need for such policing there either.

But it is in the classroom itself that the jail business does the most harm. It wholly corrupts the relationship between the teacher and the student. It makes the teacher into a mixture of taskmaster and cop. It means that, however many smiles there may be, however much the teacher may enjoy his material and want to get it across to the children, his primary function must be, by methods however subtle, to threaten and coerce. In short it makes the schoolroom into a battleground. Nothing in the way of technological or other educational devices or gimmicks can do much to change this. The results are plain. People who go into teaching full of hope and good intentions gradually become used to thinking of themselves as policemen and of the children as their natural enemies. They become cynical about their teaching and helping functions and in many cases grow, in time, to hate and despise the children they are working with. This is not their fault, and very little can be done in the way of special training or special selection to change it. It is no more possible to have open, friendly, and mutually helpful relationships between most teachers and students than it is between prison guards and prison convicts— and for exactly the same reasons. If, on the other hand, compulsory attendance were abolished, the relationship would be entirely different, for the teacher would not be a jailer, therefore not an enemy.

I have offered a number of reasons why I think compulsory school attendance is against the best interests of the schools; but I oppose it largely because I believe it is harmful and unfair to children. In speaking to many parent groups around the country, most of them in suburban areas where one might suppose the school systems to be among the best, I have heard more stories than I can remember about children being hurt and injured, and perhaps in important ways crippled, by their schools or their teachers. As a result, I have come to think that these laws are a most serious and fundamental violation of the civil liberties of the children and their parents. I believe they should be challenged—and perhaps can be overturned—on constitutional grounds. I am aware that from time to time, in various parts of the country, parents have challenged the compulsory school attendance laws, usually with no success. These challenges have been made on rather different grounds from mine—not so much that what the school was doing was bad or harmful to the child as that the parents could do as well or better at home. To this essentially elitist argument the schools have replied, reasonably enough, that the school provides certain kinds of educational resources, among them the opportunity to come in contact with large numbers of other children, that cannot be provided in the home. Their case has been strong enough so that the courts have usually been willing to uphold it. The challenge I propose is different. I say that the schools have no right to demand a child's attendance unless they are in fact helping him, that the burden of proof is on them to show, at any time, that they are in fact helping, and that where they cannot show this or where, for whatever reasons, their effects on the child are negative rather than positive, they have no right to demand that he be there. In short, though it often talks and acts as though it were, school is not the Army. The historical and legal justification for schools has been that they are good for children, every child and each child. We have not yet decided to have universal conscription for six-year-olds.

It is worth noting that when the compulsory attendance laws were enacted, they were rightly considered a pro- rather than anti-civil liberties measure. They were enacted to defend the right of children to an education against those adults who, in order to exploit them economically, would have denied it to them. The farmers and small shopkeepers and artisans of America, many of whom had not themselves had formal schooling, naturally preferred to have their children at work in the shop or mine or mill, or on the farm. The law was passed to prevent such exploitation. But times and customs have changed and the condition that the laws were passed to remedy no longer exists. There is no large market for the labor of young children; very few, if any, parents would want to keep their children home from school for economic reasons. The fact is that the only exploiters and destroyers of children today are the schools themselves.

What should the law say? It should say that if in the opinion of a child and his parents the school is doing him no good, or is indeed doing him harm, he should not be required to attend any more frequently than he wishes. There should be no burden of proof on the parents to show that they can provide facilities, companionship with other children, and all the other things the schools happen to provide. If Billy Smith hates school, and his parents feel that he is right in hating it, they are constitutionally entitled to relief. They are not obliged to demonstrate that they can give him a perfect education as against the bad one the school is giving him. It is a fundamental legal principle that if we can show that a wrong is being done, we are not compelled to say what ought to be done in its place before we are permitted to insist that it be stopped.

I know many children who find school hateful and intolerable who might discover that it was not only bearable but interesting if they were not obliged to be there every day. Even those who hate school most do not want to be away from it all the time. After all, it is where their friends are and where the action is. Many who cannot stand five days a week might actually enjoy two or three and get more education and more satisfaction than they now get out of five.

Anyone who knows anything about schools—including almost all students—recognizes that children who use any substantial part of their intelligence and energy can do in two days or less what schools ask them to do in five. If the law said that children could go to school only as much as they wanted, they would be able in nonschool time to undertake a great many serious projects for which they now have no time. It is worth noting that the eleven-year-old Rumanian girl who was the favorite of the crowd at the Olympic figure-skating championships at Grenoble in 1967 does all her studying at home. It is both interesting and sad that a Communist dictatorship should allow at least one of its children a freedom to learn that the supposedly free United States will not.

My proposal raises some thorny questions for which I do not have all the answers. What about situations in which the child and his parents do not agree about the worth or harmfulness of the school? I would say that if a child wants to go to school, and his parents do not want him to, his wish should prevail over theirs. If, on the other hand, the situation is reversed, the question is more difficult, but I would tend to put the child's wishes first. This runs counter to the prevailing and generally reasonable notion that the parents are the proper directors of a young child's life. However, I agree with Edgar Friedenberg that it is both a serious mistake and a grave injustice for our young people to have no inalienable rights of their own, with the possible exception of the right to life. (I say "possible" because I have read that there are some states in which a school may kill a child while administering "corporal punishment" without incurring any legal penalty.)

I doubt that any state legislature at the moment can be persuaded to modify the school attendance laws. I suspect that most parents value the babysitting or jailing function of the school, and that any attempt to change the laws would meet with a good deal of opposition. I think, therefore, that they must be challenged in the courts, and on the constitutional libertarian grounds that I have suggested.

I do not want to imply, however, that unless and until the courts overturn these laws, nothing can be done. One example may be cited: A nine-year-old child who attends the leading elementary school in a fairly civilized community came home in tears one day. From her first day in school this girl had been a model student. On this particular day she had had a substitute teacher in her class. She had finished a piece of assigned "seatwork" and, having nothing else to do, drew a picture of a rabbit on a small piece of paper. The teacher stole up behind her, saw the drawing, and without warning, snatched the paper and pencil away, crumpled up the paper, threw both pencil and paper against the wall, and at the top of her voice said, "If I catch you drawing another picture in class, I am going to make you write 'I shall not draw pictures in class' until your hand hurts!" The child's mother, when she heard this story after school, was furious. She called up the principal, described what had happened, and then said that although she understood why it might not be possible for him to fire the substitute teacher, she would not return her child to the class as long as this teacher was there. The principal decided to ignore the absence of the child, in my view a wise decision. In other words, a policy of resistance to the school attendance laws can perhaps achieve some results, even before the courts formally repeal or overturn them.

—1968

MAKING CHILDREN HATE READING

WHEN I WAS TEACHING English at the Colorado Rocky Mountain School, I used to ask my students the kinds of questions that English teachers usually ask about reading assignments—questions designed to bring out the points that I had decided they should know. They, on their part, would try to get me to give them hints and clues as to what I wanted. It was a game of wits. I never gave my students an opportunity to say what they really thought about a book.

I gave vocabulary drills and quizzes too. I told my students that every time they came upon a word in their book they did not understand, they were to look it up in the dictionary. I even devised special kinds of vocabulary tests, allowing them to use their books to see how the words were used. But looking back I realize that these tests, along with many of my methods, were foolish.

My sister was the first person who made me question my conventional ideas about teaching English. She had a son in the seventh grade in a fairly good public school. His teacher had asked the class to read Cooper's *The Deerslayer*. The choice was bad enough in itself; whether looking at man or nature, Cooper was superficial, inaccurate and sentimental, and his writing is ponderous and ornate. But to make matters worse, this teacher had decided to give the book the microscope and X-ray treatment. He made the students look up and memorize not only the definition but the derivation of every big word that came along—and there were plenty. Every chapter was followed by close questioning and testing to make sure the students "understood" everything.

Being then, as I said, conventional, I began to defend the teacher, who was a good friend of mine, against my sister's criticisms. The argument soon grew hot. What was wrong with making sure that children understood everything they read? My sister answered that until this class her boy had always loved reading, and had read a lot on his own; now he had stopped. (He was not really to start again for many years.)

Still I persisted. If children didn't look up the words they didn't know how would they ever learn them? My sister said, "Don't be silly! When you were little you had a huge vocabulary, and were always reading very grown-up books. When did you ever look up a word in the dictionary?"

She had me. I never looked at our dictionary. I don't use one today. In my life I doubt that I have looked up as many as fifty words, perhaps not even half that.

Since then I have talked about this with a number of teachers. More than once I have said, "According to tests, educated and literate people like you have a vocabulary of about twenty-five thousand words. How many of these did you learn by looking them up in a dictionary?" They usually are startled. Few claim to have looked up even as many as a thousand. How did they learn the rest?

They learned them just as they learned to talk: by meeting words over and over again, in different contexts, until they saw how they fitted.

Unfortunately, we English teachers are easily hung up on this matter of understanding. Why should children understand everything they read? Why should anyone? *Does* anyone? I don't, and I never did. I was always reading books that teachers would have said were "too hard" for me, books full of words I didn't know. That's how I got to be a good reader. When about ten, I read all the D'Artagnan stories and loved them. It didn't trouble me in the least that I didn't know why France was at war with England or who was quarrelling with whom in the French court or why the Musketeers should always be at odds with Cardinal Richelieu's men. I didn't even know who the Cardinal was, except that he was a dangerous and powerful man that my friends had to watch out for. This was all I needed to know.

Having said this, I will now say that I think a big, unabridged dictionary is a fine thing to have in any home or classroom. No book is more fun to browse around in—if you're not made to. Children, depending on their age, will find many pleasant and interesting things to do with a big dictionary. They can look up funny-sounding words, which they like, or words that nobody else in the class has ever heard of, which they like, or long words, which they like, or forbidden words, which they like best of all. At a certain age, and particularly with a little encouragement from parents or teachers, they may become very interested in where words came from and when they came into the language and how their meanings have changed over the years. But exploring for the fun of it is very different from looking up words out of your reading because you're going to get into trouble with your teacher if you don't.

While teaching fifth grade two years or so after the argument with my sister, I began to think about reading. The children in my class were supposed to fill out a card—just the title and author and a one-sentence summary—for every book they read. I was not running a competition to see which child could read the most books, a competition that almost always leads to cheating. I just wanted to know what the kids were reading. After a while it became clear that many of these very bright kids, from highly literate and even literary backgrounds, read very few books and deeply disliked reading. Why should this be?

At this time I was coming to realize, as I described in my book *How Children Fail,* that for most children school is a place of danger, and their main business in school is staying out of danger as much as possible. I now began to see also that books are among the most dangerous things in school.

From the very beginning of school we make books and reading a constant source of possible failure and public humiliation. When children are little we make them read aloud, before the teacher and other children, so that we can be sure they "know" all the words they are reading. This means that when they don't know a word, they are going to make a mistake, right in front of everyone. Instantly they are made to realize that they have done something wrong. Perhaps some of the other children will begin to wave their hands and say "Ooooh O-o-o-oh!" Perhaps they will just giggle, or nudge each other, or make a face. Perhaps the teacher will say, "Are you sure?" or ask someone else what he thinks. Or perhaps, if the teacher is kindly, she will just smile a sweet, sad smile—often one of the most painful punishments a child can suffer in school. In any case, the child who has made the mistake knows he has made it, and feels foolish, stupid, and ashamed, just as any of us would in his shoes.

Before long many children associate books and reading with mistakes, real or feared, and penalties and humiliation. This may not seem sensible, but it is natural. Mark Twain once said that a cat that sat on a hot stove lid would never sit on one again, but it would never sit on a cold one either. As true of children as of cats. If they, so to speak, sit on a hot book a few times, if books cause them humiliation and pain, they are likely to decide that the safest thing to do is to leave all books alone.

After having taught fifth grade classes for four years I felt quite sure of this theory. In my next class were many children who had had great trouble with schoolwork, particularly reading. I decided to try at all costs to rid them of their fear and dislike of books, and to get them to read oftener and more adventurously.

One day soon after school had started, I said to them, "Now I'm going to say something about reading that you have probably never heard a teacher say before. I would like you to read a lot of books this year, but I want you to read them only for pleasure. I am not going to ask you questions to find out whether you understand the books or not. If you understand enough of a book to enjoy it and want to go on reading it, that's enough for me. Also I'm not going to ask you what words mean.

"Finally," I said, "I don't want you to feel that just because you start a book you have to finish it. Give an author thirty or forty pages or so to get his story going. Then if you don't like the characters and you don't care what happens to them, close the book, put it away, and get another. I don't care whether the books are easy or hard, short or long, as long as you enjoy them. Furthermore I'm putting all this in a letter to your parents, so they won't feel they have to quiz and heckle you about books at home."

The children sat stunned and silent. Was this a teacher talking? One girl, who had just come to us from a school where she had had a very hard time, and who proved to be one of the most interesting, lively, and intelligent children I have ever known, looked at me steadily for a long time after I had finished. Then, still looking at me, she said slowly and solemnly, "Mr. Holt, do you really mean that?" I said just as solemnly, "I mean every word of it."

Apparently she decided to believe me. The first book she read was Dr Seuss's *How the Grinch Stole Christmas*, not a hard book even for most third graders. For a while she read a number of books on this level. Perhaps she was clearing up some confusion about reading that her teachers, in their hurry to get her up to "grade level," had never given her enough time to clear up. After she had been in the class six weeks or so and we had become good friends, I very tentatively suggested that, since she was a skillful rider and loved horses, she might like to read *National Velvet*. I made my sell as soft as possible, saying only that it was about a girl who loved and rode horses, and that if she didn't like it she could put it back. She tried it, and though she must have found it quite a bit harder than what she had been reading, finished it and liked it very much.

During the spring she really astounded me, however. One day, in one of our many free periods, she was reading at her desk. From a glimpse of the illustrations I thought I knew what the book was. I said to myself, "It can't be," and went to take a closer look. Sure enough, she was reading *Moby Dick*, in the edition with the woodcuts by Rockwell Kent. When I came closer to her desk she looked up. I said, "Are you really reading that?" She said she was. I said, "Do you like it?" She said, "Oh, yes, it's neat!" I said, "Don't you find parts of it rather heavy going?" She answered, "Oh, sure, but I just skip over those parts and go on to the next good part."

This is exactly what reading should be and in school so seldom is—an exciting, joyous adventure. Find something, dive into it, take the good parts, skip the bad parts, get what you can out of it; go on to something else. How different is our mean-spirited, picky insistence that every child get every last little scrap of "understanding" that can be dug out of a book?

For teachers who really enjoy doing it, and will do it with gusto, reading aloud is a very good idea. I have found that not just fifth graders but even ninth and eleventh graders enjoy it. Jack London's *To Build a Fire* is a good read-aloud story. So are spooky stories: "August Heat" by W. F. Harvey and "The Monkey's Paw" by W. W. Jacobs are among the best. Shirley Jackson's "The Lottery" is sure-fire, and will raise all kinds of questions for discussion and argument. Because of a TV program they had seen and that had excited them, I once started reading my fifth graders William Golding's *Lord of the Flies*, thinking to read only a few chapters, but they made me read it to the end.

In my early fifth grade classes the children usually were of high IQ, came from literate backgrounds, and were generally felt to be succeeding in school. Yet it was astonishingly hard for most of those children to express themselves in speech or in writing. I have known a number of five-year-olds who were considerably more articulate than most of the fifth graders I have known in school. Asked to speak, my fifth graders were overcome with embarrassment; many refused altogether. Asked to write, they would sit for minutes on end, staring at the paper. It was hard for most of them to get down a half page of writing, even on what seemed to be interesting topics or topics they chose themselves.

In desperation I hit on a device that I named the Composition Derby. I divided the class into teams, and told them that when I said, "Go," they were to start writing something. It could be about anything they wanted, but it had to be about something: they couldn't just write "dog dog dog dog" on the paper. It could be true stories, descriptions of people or places or events, wishes, made-up stories, dreams—anything they liked. Spelling didn't count, so they didn't have to worry about it. When I said, "Stop," they were to stop and count up the words they had written. The team that wrote the most words would win the derby.

It was a success in many ways and for many reasons. The first surprise was that the two children who consistently wrote the most words were two of the least successful students in the class. They were bright, but they had always had a very hard time in school. Both were very bad spellers, and worrying about this had slowed down their writing without improving their spelling. When they were free of this worry and could let themselves go, they found hidden and unsuspected talents.

One of the two, a very driven and anxious little boy, used to write long adventures, or misadventures, in which I was the central character: "The Day Mr. Holt Went to Jail," "The Day Mr. Holt Fell into the Hole," "The Day Mr. Holt Got Run Over," and so on. These were very funny, and the class enjoyed hearing me read them aloud. One day I asked the class to write a derby on a topic I would give them. They groaned: they liked picking their own. "Wait till you hear it," I said. "It's 'The Day the School Burned Down.'"

With a shout of approval and joy they went to work, and wrote furiously for twenty minutes or more, laughing and chuckling as they wrote. The papers were all much alike; in them the children danced around the burning building, throwing in books and driving me and the other teachers back in when we tried to escape.

In our first derby the class wrote an average of about ten words a minute; after a few months their average was over twenty. Some of the slower writers tripled their output. Even the slowest, one of whom was the best student in the class, were writing fifteen words a minute. More important, almost all the children enjoyed the derbies and wrote interesting things.

Some time later I learned that Professor S. I. Hayakawa, teaching freshman English, had invented a better technique. Every day in class he asked his students to write without stopping for about half an hour. They could write on whatever topic or topics they chose; the important thing was not to stop. If they ran dry, they were to copy their last sentence over and over again until new ideas came. Usually they came before the sentence had been copied once. I use this idea in my own classes, and call this kind of paper a Non-Stop. Sometimes I ask students to write a Non-Stop on an assigned topic, more often on anything they choose. [Now, (Winter 1969) my students at Berkeley do about ten to fifteen minutes of this private writing in almost every class—and I with them. We all find our thoughts coming much faster than we can write them, and ever more so with practice. Many students have said they enjoy this very much.] Once in a while I ask them to count up how many words they have written, though I rarely ask them to tell me; it is for their own information.

Sometimes these papers are to be handed in; often they are what I call private papers, for the students' eyes alone.

The private paper has proved very useful. In the first place, in any English class—certainly any large English class—if the amount students write is limited by what the teacher can find time to correct, or even to read, the students will not write nearly enough. The remedy is to have them write a great deal that the teacher does not read. In the second place, students writing for themselves will write about many things that they would never write on a paper to be handed in, once they have learned (sometimes it takes a while) that the teacher means what he says about the papers' being private. This is important, not just because it enables them to get things off their chest, but also because they are most likely to write well, and to pay attention to how they write, when they are writing about something important to them.

Some English teachers, when they first hear about private papers, object that students do not benefit from writing papers unless the papers are corrected. I disagree for several reasons. First, most students, particularly poor students, do not read the corrections on their papers; it is boring, even painful. Second, even when they do read these corrections, they do not get much help from them, do not build the teacher's suggestions into their writing. This is true even when they really believe the teacher knows what he is talking about.

Third, and most important, we learn to write by writing, not by reading other people's ideas about writing. What most students need above all else is practice in writing, and particularly in writing about things that matter to them, so that they will begin to feel the satisfaction that comes from getting important thoughts down in words and will care about stating these thoughts forcefully and clearly.

Teachers of English—or, as some schools say (ugh!), Language Arts—spend a lot of time and effort on spelling. Most of it is wasted; it does little good, and often more harm than good. We should ask ourselves, "How do good spellers spell? What do they do when they are not sure which spelling of a word is right?" I have asked this of a number of good spellers. Their answer never varies. They do not rush for a dictionary or rack their brains trying to remember rules. They write down the word both ways or several ways, look at them, and pick the one that looks best. Usually they are right.

Good spellers know what words look like and even, in their writing muscles, feel like. They have a good set of word images in their minds and are willing to trust these images. The things we do to "teach" spelling to children do little to develop these skills or talents, and much to destroy them or prevent them from developing.

The first and worst thing we do is to make children anxious about spelling. We treat a misspelled word like a crime and penalize the misspeller severely; many teachers talk of making children develop a "spelling conscience," and fail otherwise excellent papers because of a few spelling mistakes. This approach is self-defeating. When we are anxious, we don't perceive clearly or remember what we once perceived. Everyone knows how hard it is to recall even simple things when under emotional pressure; the harder we rack our brains, the less easy it is to find what we are looking for. If we are anxious enough, we will not trust the messages that memory sends us. Many children spell badly because although their first hunch about how to spell a word may be correct, they are afraid to trust it. I have often seen on children's papers a word correctly spelled, then crossed out and misspelled.

There are some tricks that might help children get sharper word images. Some teachers may be using them. One is the trick of air writing; that is, of "writing" a word in the air with a finger and "seeing" the image so formed. I did this quite a bit with fifth graders, using either the air or the top of a desk, on which the fingers left no mark. Many of them were tremendously excited by this. I can still hear them saying, "There's nothing there, but I can see it!" It seemed like magic. I remember that when I was little I loved to write in the air. It was effortless, voluptuous, and satisfying, and it was fun to see the word appear in the air. I used to write "Money Money Money," not so much because I didn't have any as because I liked the way it felt, particularly that *y* at the end, with its swooping tail.

Another thing to help sharpen children's image-making machinery is taking very quick looks at words—or other things. The conventional machine for doing this is the tachistoscope. But these are expensive, so expensive that most children can have few chances to use them, if any at all. With some three-by-five and four-by-eight file cards you can get the same effect. On the little cards you put the words or the pictures that the child is going to look at. You hold the larger card over the card to be read, uncover it for a split second with a quick wrist motion, then cover it up again. Thus you have a tachistoscope that costs one cent and that any child can work by himself.

Once when substituting in a first grade class I thought that the children, who were just beginning to read and write, might enjoy some of the kind of free, nonstop writing that my fifth graders had. About forty minutes before lunch, I asked them all to take pencil and paper and start writing about anything they wanted. They seemed to like the idea, but right away one child said anxiously, "Suppose we can't spell a word?"

"Don't worry about it." I said. "Just spell it the best way you can."

A heavy silence settled on the room. All I could see were still pencils and anxious faces. This was clearly not the right approach. So I said, "All right, I'll tell you what to do. Any time you want to know how to spell a word, tell me and I'll write it on the board."

They breathed a sigh of relief and went to work. Soon requests for words were coming fast; as soon as I wrote one, someone asked me another. By lunchtime, when most of the children were still busily writing, the board was full. What was interesting was that most of the words they had asked for were much longer and more complicated than anything in their reading books or workbooks. Freed from worry about spelling, they were willing to use the most difficult and interesting words that they knew.

The words were still on the board when we began school next day. Before I began to erase them, I said to the children, "Listen, everyone, I have to erase these words, but before I do, just out of curiosity I'd like to see if you remember some of them."

The result was surprising. I had expected that the child who had asked for and used a word might remember it, but I did not think that many others would. But many of the children still knew many of the words. How had they learned them? I suppose each time I wrote a word on the board a number of children had looked up, relaxed yet curious, just to see what the word looked like, and these images and the sound of my voice saying the word had stuck in their minds until the next day. This, it seems to me, is how children may best learn to write and spell.

What can a parent do if a school, or a teacher, is spoiling the language for a child by teaching it in some tired old way? First, try to get them to change, or at least let them know that you are eager for change. Talk to other parents: push some of the ideas in the PTA; talk to the English department at the school; talk to the child's own teacher. Many teachers and schools want to know what the parents want.

If the school or teacher cannot be persuaded, then what? Perhaps all you can do is try not to let your child become too bored or discouraged or worried by what is happening in school. Help him meet the school's demands, foolish though they may seem, and try to provide more interesting alternatives at home—plenty of books and conversation, and a serious and respectful audience when a child wants to talk. Nothing that ever happened to me in English classes at school was as helpful to me as the long conversations I used to have every summer with my uncle, who made me feel that the difference in our ages was not important and that he was really interested in what I had to say.

At the end of her freshman year in college a girl I knew wrote home to her mother, "Hooray! Hooray! Just think—I never have to take English any more!" But this girl had always been an excellent English student, had always loved books, writing, ideas. It seems unnecessary and foolish and wrong that English teachers should so often take what should be the most flexible, exciting, and creative of all school courses and make it into something that most children can hardly wait to see the last of. Let's hope that we can and soon will begin to do much better.

—1967

ORDER AND DISORDER

THE FOLLOWING ARE SOME slightly abridged and edited excerpts from a letter sent to the *Yale Alumni Magazine*, in reply to an article published by it about teaching in ghetto schools.

Our schools are hung up on the notion that learning in the classroom is a by-product of order. In fact, it is the other way around. Children will raise hell in a classroom if, as is usually the case, there is nothing better to do. At least, they will want to. The docile ones will be afraid to; the ones like most of our city kids, who have nothing to fear or gain from society, will not hesitate. And true learning is not an orderly process to begin with.

A teacher says, "I did not know what books to use, how to pronounce some of their names, what to put on the bulletin boards, what to do with the four children who spoke only Spanish, or how to make my handwriting on the blackboard anything more than an illegible scrawl." These are real problems, but are the answers to them so hard to find? Books? Why not find out whether any of the children have ever read any books they like, or whether there are things they are interested in: why not, for a start, bring in some books by black writers? This has worked wherever it has been tried. Pronouncing names? Why not ask them? Bulletin boards? Why not post anything that seems interesting? There is not an issue of *Life* or *Look* magazine, to name only two, that doesn't have at least one, usually at least twenty interesting pictures in it. Spanish speaking children? Why not start learning some Spanish so as to talk to them? After all, if they are expected to learn English in one year, their teacher ought to be able to learn Spanish. Anyway, they can at least meet in the middle.

Handwriting? Why not print? Or practice? Or let the children in on the secret that a good many adults don't have very good handwriting, and confront it as a joint problem?

Later he talks about "tacit group strategy." And again, "when the children are testing how much control they can gain over a classroom." This is popular mythology among school teachers. It is nonsense. What children want is not to gain control over a classroom, but to get out of it. They do what they do because they hate the classroom and because the things they are asked to do there are boring and stupid. They resist being made to stand in pointless lines for the same reason that any sensible human being does. There are times, as in waiting for a bus or at a ticket window, when a line is a functional arrangement. It makes sure that the first to come are the first to get served. But for getting from one place to another, like out of a building, a line makes no sense at all. A veteran teacher in a school in a Philadelphia slum told me not long ago that though the school "requires" lines, she has ignored this requirement for years. She has her children get ready to go home, sits them at their desks, and then lets them out, sometimes singly, sometimes in groups of four or five, depending upon the amount of ruckus they are liable to kick up on the way. They know that the system is more practical and they cooperate with her in making it work. If they make a big fuss, someone is going to complain and there will be trouble all around. They don't make a fuss. They are not interested in a contest with her; they are interested, just as she is, in getting out of the place and going home. Children are sensible people if we give them half a chance to act as if they were.

The teacher's job was certainly not made any easier by the marvelously incompetent school administration that was not even able to tell him during the summer what grades he would be teaching in the fall. But he says, "since I knew so little about what the children needed to learn I chose lessons I thought I could teach." Did he really think that the latter had nothing to do with the former? Plenty of teachers do.

Spelling? The place to get spelling words is from the children's own writing. If the children are not writing, are not interested enough in anything to be able to write about it, then there is the first problem, not spelling. He says the children could not read books on a sixth grade level. How can one be sure of this? We know now that many children our city schools have solemnly pronounced unable to read are in fact reading adult books like the *Autobiography of Malcolm X*, *The Fire Next Time*, and so forth. The trick is to put before the child books or magazines, or articles, or newspaper stories that he wants to find out about. He will do the rest. If he wants help, he will come looking for it.

He describes a good lesson that was interrupted when "one of the Spanish-speaking boys who did not understand a word of what we were saying, decided that it was time to clean out his desk." Chances are that what he decided was that it was time to put an end to this animated discussion in which he could not take part. Later a math lesson was interrupted by a fire truck. Is the lesson plan really so sacred? Are fire trucks, fire prevention, fires, and indeed the organization of government that makes fire prevention possible not worthy of discussion? Why not seize opportunities as they come? Fires cost money. How much do they cost? How much do firemen get paid? What would be a fair wage for a fireman? What should a man be paid who risks his life? What would the kids ask in order to be firemen? What should the family of a fireman get if he is killed? How much does it cost a family to live? And so on.

He says, "it took me far too long to realize that some of my children were refusing to remove their jackets in seventy-degree room temperature because they were embarrassed to reveal the rips and tears in blouses and shorts." More credit to him for realizing this, but why is it the teacher's business to tell his students to take off their coats at all? I lecture to a good many groups and I would not think of beginning by telling them what to do with their coats. That is their business and they would quite rightly be offended if I stuck my nose into it. Why, in this matter, can we not treat children with the same respect and courtesy that we would offer to any other human being?

So his pupils told him that he had to hit them to make them good. I don't doubt it for a second. People have been telling them that for years. But that does not make it true, and we ought to know that it is not true, and that those who had those children think it was true have done them a most serious injustice and injury. He says later that he decided that what these children needed was to be treated with respect. But his definition of respect is most extraordinary. He seems to say that to respect somebody is to give him orders, reward him if he carries them out and punish him if he does not—in short, to treat him like a slave, not an equal. What these children needed was what they have never had, a very different kind of respect which a teacher could best show them by treating them as if they were, or could soon become, reasonable and sensible human beings. To respect someone is to trust him and to make clear that you do.

He tells with obvious satisfaction how he was able to get one boy to get ready at the beginning of the lesson by one day picking up his desk and dumping its contents on the floor. I find this story contemptible and indeed outrageous. To the reply, "Well, it worked," I can only say that lots of things "work." As far as getting things done is concerned, Nazi Germany "worked." He might have done better to ask himself for a while why any Puerto Rican boy living in New York and in his right mind *would* spend much time listening to someone talk about the Pharaohs of ancient Egypt. The example shows better than anything I could pick the triviality and irrelevance of the kind of so-called education being thrust at these children. Small wonder that they pay little attention. He says, "At the beginning of the year the thought of ripping up sloppy notebooks, breaking pencils, dumping desks on the floor would have seemed like acts of blatant teacher brutality." But that is precisely what they were, and if, as he says, the children wanted it, assuming that they really did, it was because they had never known anything else. Might it not be our job to introduce them to something different and better? Might it not be a good idea to wean these children from an unthinking dependence on authority, to get them to give up their submissive-rebellious role, and start to think and act like reasonable and independent human beings?

The matter of children's writing in Harlem has been so thoroughly and eloquently covered by Herbert Kohl in his book *36 Children* that I will not take it up here, except to say that anyone who thinks that these children are "communications cripples" because they cannot or do not speak standard English is making a most serious mistake. A great deal of nonsense has been written about the inability of slum children to talk. I, and people well known to me, have seen enough of these children in favorable circumstances to know that they can talk very competently and expressively when they have something to talk about and someone they trust to talk to. Not that it is easy to get them to feel this trust, but one will never do it if one thinks that the most important thing to teach them is to put capital letters at the start of sentences and periods at the end. If we want to help semiliterate children become good writers, that is not the place to start.

What keeps most teachers from achieving good communication in the classroom is their feeling that when children do not speak as we do, it means that they are in some important way inferior. Last summer I attended a small meeting of Upward Bound students at Yale. For several hours these teenage boys, dredged up from the very bottom of the school barrel, told a small group of adults what had been wrong with their schooling. What was astonishing, indeed scarcely believable, was the way in which these boys changed their style of talking as they became increasingly convinced that we their hearers really wanted to hear what they had to say, and were judging neither their opinions nor their way of expressing them. They began by talking in an almost incomprehensible slang; by the end of the meeting they were speaking both effectively and in something quite close to standard English. Nor is this the first time I have seen this happen. At a meeting of the Lower East Side Action Project (LEAP) in New York I heard teenagers of Puerto Rican parentage telling a group of adults about their problems, hopes, and ambitions. No one hearing these young men, most of them school dropouts, could claim for a second that they were unable to use language powerfully and expressively. Indeed, their use of language put to shame a good many of the supposedly educated people at the meeting.

By the end of his paper this teacher shows that he sensed much of what I am saying. Thus he says, "but any time I managed to reach their interests, curiosity spilled forth and their faces glowed with enthusiasm. I brought a copy of the *Autobiography of Malcolm X* to class and mentioned that Malcolm had spent much of his early life in the streets six or seven blocks from our school. After less than a paragraph they were jumping with questions and comments: "Did he really teach himself to read without any teacher?" "What did he look like?" "Why did he get shot?" It sounds as though the communication barrier of which so many teachers speak had suddenly disappeared. Later he says, "The children could sense that I was not handing them a carefully prepared package, and *responded as though they knew that their ideas made some difference.*" Let me repeat that last—responded as though they knew that their ideas made some difference. This is what respect means, not turning people's desks upside down and ripping up their notebooks. It means treating them as if their ideas made some difference, and when we treat people this way, whatever their age, color, or background, we find that communication barriers disappear and that learning takes place. This is, of course, what ought to be happening everywhere in our schools—at Yale as much as in Harlem—and so seldom happens anywhere.

—1968

Teaching the Unteachable

A few years ago, when the poverty program got under way and we began to rediscover our poor, there was a rush of articles about the children growing up in our city's slums. They proved to be strange, silent creatures indeed. We were told that they didn't know the names of things, didn't know that things had names, didn't even know their own names. We were told that, having never heard any real speech, they could hardly speak more than occasional monosyllables themselves. The people who reported these things were serious, and sympathetic, and sincerely believed every word they said; and I, like many other people, believed them.

How do you find out, anyway, whether a child knows his own name? Smiling kindly at him, and speaking in a gentle and reassuring tone of voice, you ask him, "What's your name?" If he doesn't answer, it presumably shows that he doesn't know. Or perhaps, knowing his name, you call him by it. If, hearing his name, he makes no move or reply; again it shows that he doesn't know it. Simple.

Only, as Mr. Kohl has shown, and by now some others as well, it may not be so simple. It makes a certain kind of sense to try to judge what a child knows by seeing what he can do, but that leaves out the possibility that he may choose not to show what he can do, that he may decide that at school the safest course is to say and do as little as possible, at least until he knows what and who this strange place and these strange people are.

I am suddenly reminded of Submarine Officers' Training School in New London in the fall of 1943. Here we sat, 270 student officers, and there up in front were our teachers, ex-sub-skippers yanked away from the Pacific and their chances for heroism, fame, and advancement. "We want to know who you are," they told us. "If you see us in the bar at the Officer's Club, come up and introduce yourself, and we'll have some talk." Some students took this advice. How friendly and welcoming was the submarine service? How pleasant and salty and exciting were these veteran skippers? Yes; but they were also, to a man, sore as hell about being in New London instead of the Pacific, and when, in class or on a training ship or wherever, their anger and impatience could not be contained, the students who got it in the neck were very likely to be the ones whose names they knew. They never knew mine; when I graduated, 13th in the class, the only officer who knew me by name was the school Exec, from whom I had had to get permission to leave on weekends. My caution paid off handsomely. It should not surprise us if slum children, finding themselves in a place where most of the grown-ups neither look nor sound like anyone they know, are equally cautious.

There is no need to set forth here the many ways in which the schools of our city slums are in most cases an environment fiercely and unrelievedly hostile and destructive to the children who attend them. That story has been told in part by Mr. Kohl, and will be told many times again. I would like to stress here a somewhat different point. From Mr. Kohl's book we could easily get the impression that he is talking about a special problem: how to make disadvantaged children articulate and literate. In fact the problem is much wider. Our so-called best schools are turning out students most of whom, in any real and important sense, are as inarticulate as the most deprived children of the ghettos, as little able to speak or write simply and directly about things of importance to them, what they know, want, and care about. The training in writing that they get, unless they are very lucky, is largely training in bull-slinging and snowjobbery. Every year students at all levels write millions of papers. It is a safe bet that most of the times—I would guess over 95 percent—the writers of these papers do not care about and in fact have no honest and genuine opinions about what they are writing, and would not write the paper if they were not made to. I once asked a very able high school senior, a straight A student in English, if she ever kept any of her old

English papers. She looked at me amazed. "For heaven's sake," she said, "what for?"

What for, indeed? And a senior, soon to graduate Cum Laude from one of the leading Ivy League colleges, told me not long ago—and I have to add that he was no radical or troublemaker—that he and everyone he knew were wholly convinced that their surest chance of getting an A on their papers and in their courses was to repeat the professor's ideas back to him, though of course in somewhat altered language.

It would be easy to compile a bookful of horror stories about schools and classrooms where neatness, mechanical accuracy, and orthodoxy of opinion—i.e., agreeing with the teacher's spoken or even unspoken notions of what is right and proper for children to believe and say—count for far more than honest, independent, original expression. It is still common in a great many schools to fail papers that have more than a very few errors in grammar, punctuation, or spelling, regardless of any other merit they might have. Not long ago I talked to the mother of an eight- or nine-year-old whose most recent paper, entirely free of any mechanical errors and otherwise (as the teacher admitted) well written, was failed because he wrote it in three colors of ink. And this was in a "good" school system. But the real reason that our schools do not turn out people who can use language simply and strongly, let alone beautifully, lies deeper. It is that with very few exceptions the schools, from kindergarten through graduate school, do not give a damn what the students think. Think, care about, or want to know. What counts is what the system has decided they shall be made to learn. Teachers' manuals for the elementary and even secondary grades instruct teachers to have "discussions" in which they "bring out the following points." What kind of a discussion is that?

If we are to make real progress in improving student writing, the first lesson we have to learn is this: a student will be concerned with his own use of language, will care about its effectiveness, and therefore try to judge its effectiveness, only when he is talking to an audience, and not just one that allows him to say what he wants as he wants, but one that takes him and his ideas seriously. This does not mean letting him take a shot at expressing his thoughts so that we teachers can then demolish them or show how much better are our own. In this respect the so-called and perhaps misnamed Socratic method is not only dishonest but destructive. It is easy for even half-smart adults to win arguments with children who are unskilled at arguing, or to lead them into logical traps and pitfalls. Children so outplayed at the word game will after a while simply stop playing it, or will concentrate on playing it our way. What we have to recognize is something quite different, that it is the effort to use words well, to say what he wants to say, to people whom he trusts and wants to reach and move, that alone will teach a young person to use words better. No doubt, given this starting point, some technical advice and help may at times be useful; but we must begin from here or we will make no progress at all.

A final question. What difference does it make? Above all, what difference does it make whether the children of our poor, and notably our poor blacks, learn to speak and write well or not? Should we not bend all our efforts to giving them the kind of training that will enable them to get jobs and do work that will lift them, at least a little, out of their poverty? The answer is that this is nowhere near enough. It is of the greatest importance to our society that the children of our poor, particularly if they are black, shall be skillful in the use of words. Not just skillful enough to be able to read signs and instructions, but skillful enough to be able to reach, instruct, and move other men. For our society faces a choice. Either we become a genuinely integrated society, in which the color of a man's skin has no more to do with the way other men treat him and feel about him than, say, the color of his eyes or his hair, or we will become a genuinely, whole-heartedly, unashamedly racist society, like that of Nazi Germany or present South Africa—with perhaps our own Final Solution waiting at the end. In short, either we whites get cured of our racism, and fairly soon, or it will kill all of whatever decent is left in our society. One thing that might help cure us is a black population articulate enough to make us feel what racism is like for those who suffer under it. No doubt we have some black spokesmen today, but they are so few—too few, and too remote. What a few Baldwins, Kings and Carmichaels now tell us, we need to be told by thousands, hundreds of thousands. Enough blacks, with enough words, might break down our often unspoken and even unconscious feeling that they are different, inferior, despicable, even terrifying, and awaken instead in us an awareness of our common humanity, and their pain, and our responsibility for it. And while they are doing that, they might at the same time organize and educate themselves, and their allies among the other poor and dispossessed, into a political force strong and effective enough to make some of the changes we need to make our society, in Paul Goodman's words, not Great, but only decent, a society in which all men can live without hate, fear, or guilt.

—1967

EDUCATION FOR THE FUTURE

I WRITE ABOUT WHAT I THINK
ought to happen, not what is likely to happen. We must hope for the
best; but it does not look right now as if man is smart enough, far-
seeing enough, generous enough, or trusting enough, to get himself
out of the difficulties he has made and keeps on making for himself.

Secondly, I write knowing how risky it is to talk about the future.
During World War II we were told many times that in the Postwar
World of Tomorrow, every American—every decent, prosperous
American, at least—would have his own helicopter out in the back
yard, ready to whisk him wherever he wished. It hasn't happened, and
it almost certainly won't. Many other predictions have proved equally wrong.

Thirdly, words being what they are, I must write about the problems of the future as if they were more or less separate and unrelated,
taking them one at a time in some order, whereas in fact they are tied
together, all of a piece. To take only one example, I must talk about
the problem of work as if it had relatively little to do with the problems of racism or peace, but the fact is that the increasing scarcity,
uncertainty, and dullness of work, for many people at least, will arouse
in them anxieties and resentments that will make the problems of
racism and peace much harder to deal with. In the same way, the
problem of population is made more difficult by the fact of racism: in
many parts of the world the essentially well-meant efforts of the prosperous West to help poor people reduce their birth rate are seen, and
therefore resisted, as an attempt by whites to keep down the numbers
of blacks, the better to keep them under control.

Also, as long as we continue to measure military success in Vietnam by the number of dead bodies we can count, we can hardly blame other poor countries for feeling that their best defense against our violent meddling in their affairs may be to have as many live bodies as they can.

Hundreds of similar interconnections can be found. The many problems we seem to face are in fact part of a whole problem. Unfortunately, we cannot say what the whole problem is, except by talking about all the parts that make it up.

How shall we list them? It seems best to list first problems that embrace and concern the whole world: peace and racism, then problems that more particularly concern our own society: work and leisure, waste and the environment, and freedom. Some may feel at this point that I have wandered off the subject. Under education, one might expect to find talk about crowded classrooms, shortages of teachers, outmoded buildings, antiquated forms of fiscal support, the full academic year, the impact of educational technology, etc. I have left these subjects out, because to me they are problems of educational institutions, not education. They are means, not ends. The problem before us is not how shall schools do their job, but what is their job, what has education to do with the great issues and problems of our times?

Peace

More and more, we are coming to believe that peace can be maintained, or at least nuclear war avoided or prevented, by nuclear stalemate or "balance of terror." And indeed the stalemate has "worked" better than most people, certainly most peace workers, ever thought it would. But it would be a dangerous mistake to feel that we can rely on it indefinitely, and that we have no real need to make radical changes in the way we run the world and deal with its problems and differences. There are three reasons for this. One is that technology may at any moment destroy this stalemate. Another has been frequently stated: that the nuclear stalemate will grow more unstable as more nations get nuclear weapons and delivery systems. We cannot be sure that the Chinese, or, some day, the Indians and Pakistanis, or, some day, the Israelis and the Arab states, or, some day, the black-ruled and white-ruled nations of Africa, will be as cautious with their nuclear weapons as the Russians have been. The third reason has hardly been stated at all. The nuclear stalemate is given all the credit for keeping the United States and Russia out of war, but the most important reason that we have not fought is that we do not have and never did have anything really worth fighting about. The quarrel between us was from the start an unreal one, not based on real issues, but on the suddenly inflamed fears and suspicions of our leaders.

I remember an article that appeared in the *Reader's Digest*, not long after the end of World War II. It was called something like, "Why There Will Be Peace between the U.S. and Russia." It pointed out that neither nation had anything, territories or resources, that the other really needed or wanted; that we had no adjoining boundaries where disputes could heat up into open fighting; that our interests and, in most important respects, our aims and outlooks were far more alike than opposed. The article was right. The quarrel that grew out of passion died down, or at least became manageable, when those passions cooled off.

The chief danger of a World War III lies elsewhere. It will not grow less with time. It does not lie in men who have become momentarily angry at and fearful of each other, but in problems and differences that are not imagined but real, and that time will make not better but worse. For the world of 1969 is, to a very large degree, two worlds. Most of the people in the world live in one; they are black and very poor; and every year they grow poorer. In the other world live the rest of us, a rich white minority. This alone would be cause enough for friction; but there are others. Much of the wealth we enjoy we took, by force or fraud, from black peoples; they are beginning to want it back, and we are not ready to give it back. Moreover, that part of the world's resources that we consume grows year by year; we grow richer as the others grow poorer. Finally, and perhaps most serious of all, we rich whites are racists. Most of us, in varying degrees, despise, fear, and hate people of any color other than our own.

Clearly this is not a situation that will improve with time. It will not even stand still. If all the black nations were as poor and disorganized as some of the newer African states, we might hope for some time, perhaps a very long time, to keep them poor, ignorant, and pow-erless, as the white South Africans have kept down their black major-ity. But this is not the case. There is China; and even without China, some of the others would and will some day have their own atomic and, probably, chemical and bacteriological weapons. Hence the dan-ger of a great, worldwide race war—perhaps sudden and nuclear, per-haps a long, dreadful, barbarous extension of our present bloodbath in Vietnam.

To prevent this, to get a stable and long-lasting peace, we cannot go on as we are, relying on luck and the nuclear stalemate. We must end racism, make a fairer distribution of the world's resources, make a serious attack on poverty, gather up and destroy most or all of the world's arsenal of weapons of mass destruction, and devise and put into action more just and rational ways of dealing with world-wide problems and settling international disputes. These tasks will all take a long time, and I don't mean to say that world peace must wait on their completion. But they must be seriously begun.

What has education to do with this task? It seems easy to say that we must use our schools to produce a generation and more of citizens who will understand that these things must be done, and a certain body of experts who will have the skills to do them. But this is only the least part of the task; the real job is altogether different. It has lit-tle or nothing to do with content, curricula, or learning, and a great deal to do with the human heart and spirit. Once, in an essay called "Education and Peace," I wrote:

Our efforts for peace are doomed to fail unless we understand that the root causes of war are...the kind of men who must have and will find scapegoats, legitimate targets for the disappointment, envy, fear, rage, and hatred that accumulate in their daily lives. The man who hates or despises his work, his boss, his neighbors, and above all himself, will find a way to make other men suffer and die for his own missing sense of freedom, competence, dignity, and worth.

The fundamental educational problem of our time is to find ways to help children grow into adults who have no wish to do harm. We must recognize that traditional education, far from having ever solved this problem, has never tried to solve it. Indeed, its efforts have, if any-thing, been in exactly the opposite direction. An important aim of traditional education has always been to make children into the kind of adults who were ready to hate and kill whomever their leaders might declare to be their enemies. But even those societies that did not set out to make their children warlike, jingoistic, xenophobic, ready to see every stranger as an enemy, have never tried to make them feel that the moral code that governs their relations with their neighbors reaches out to include all of mankind.

The fact is that all the moral codes by which men have lived have contained an escape clause, sometimes implied, but often clearly stated. In one way or another these codes have said what our Ten Commandments say: thou shalt not kill, thou shalt not steal, thou shalt not covet, thou shalt not bear false witness, and so on. But then they add a footnote, that these rules only apply when you are talking about Us—Our Tribe, Our Kingdom, Our Faith. When we start talking about Them, those people on the outside, strangers, heathen, unbelievers, then the moral code goes out the window, and everything is allowed. Lie, steal, cheat, kill, destroy, torture—nothing is too bad; in fact, the worse, the better. [When I wrote this, we had not yet begun to drop napalm and white phosphorus on men, women, and children in peasant villages in Vietnam. I had not thought, somehow, that we would go so far.]

Human society has never until now had to come to grips with the source of human evil-doing, which is the wish to do evil.... The moral codes worked, at least fairly well, within their limited frames of reference, precisely because there always were people whom it was all right to hate and injure as much as you wished. And mankind was able to afford the escape clause, was able to survive the destruction of his enemies that his moral code allowed him, because his means of destruction were so limited, and because it took most of his time and energy just to keep alive...

But no more.... The means to kill tens and hundreds of millions of people, even to destroy all life on earth, lie ready to hand. And cheap to boot. The man who does not value his own life, and hence feels that no life has value, may not be able to make Doomsday machines in his own basement, but with the vote, or even without it, he can get his government to make them and eventually to use them. We do not, in fact, need even this much will to do evil, to accomplish the destruction of mankind. It will take heroic efforts, supported by an undreamed-of willingness to risk, trust, and sacrifice, to collect and destroy all the weapons of mass destruction that have already been made, and to ensure that no more such weapons will ever be made again. Those who are not ready and determined to do this have only to hang back, to obstruct, to keep us going along as we are, in order to ensure the end of the world.

Against this background and in this light, the argument of A. S. Neill of Summerhill, that the business of education is above all else to make happy people, must be seen to be, not frivolous and sentimental, but in the highest degree serious, weighty, and to the point. For the sake of man's survival we must indeed learn to make people who will want and will be able to live lives that are full, meaningful, and joyous. This means that we must give children, at home and in school, what few of them now have—freedom, dignity, and respect.

In other words, what we most need to work effectively for peace is not more of this or that kind of learning, but more of certain qualities of mind and heart. The rich nations are doing less and less each year to help the development of the poor nations, not because they don't know enough, but because they don't care enough. What we lack is not technology or resources, but sympathy and generosity. And these are not developed in school by telling children how important they are, or making them, under threat of punishment and disgrace, "share" everything they own with anyone who happens to ask for it. They will be developed only by creating in the school an atmosphere of freedom, respect, and trust, within which true kindness and generosity can be expected to grow.

Racism

Racism, as we are beginning to see both in England and Russia, is a serious problem and threat in many parts of the rich white world. There may well be no white nations in which it does not exist, ready to break out and show itself if enough black people appear. It is particularly serious here in the United States, not because we are the most racist of countries—we are not—but because we are the most rich and powerful. The question is, what can we do in the field of education to help get rid of racism? The Supreme Court, almost all non-racist whites, and almost all blacks agree on the answer: integrate the schools. [This was written in 1965. Times have changed.] I feel more urgently than many that we must. But my reasons for feeling so may be somewhat unusual.

Almost every believer in integrated education, asked why schools should be integrated, would say, in effect, "Because otherwise black people cannot get equal education." I doubt that this is the most important reason, and I'm not sure that it is even true. It is for the sake of our white children, not our black, that we most need integration. Racism, at least in this country, at least so far, is a disease of white men, not of black. Since the disease is one that, if it runs long enough, will destroy our freedom and, by leading us into race war, perhaps our lives, we must cure ourselves of it. There is probably no way to do that but to raise a generation or two free of it, and there is no way to do that but to make sure that all white children, as they grow up, come into frequent and prolonged contact with black children. When we see the problem this way, it does not seem any more that our troubles arise from having too many black children; the real problem may be that we don't have enough black children.

But I am by no means sure that integrated education will be the best for most blacks. It seems to me that relations between white America and black America have long been, and are still, exactly like those between a rich colonial power and a poor, undeveloped, exploited colony with this odd difference—that the two countries happen to be occupying the same territory. For many years, and most particularly in recent years, the blacks have been trying, in effect, to get the whites to let them leave the colony and migrate to the mother country, to leave black America and move into white America. With few exceptions, the effort has failed, and has largely come to an end. Blacks are beginning to face the fact that they are not going to be allowed to leave their undeveloped country. Their only alternative, then, is to develop it. But it is by no means sure that the kind of education they will or might receive in integrated schools will best prepare them for this task.

An example comes to mind. Of all the books written during World War II about what might be called world politics, the only one

I know of that was not almost instantly dated by events, and in fact the best such book I have ever read, is Edmond Taylor's *Richer By Asia*. It should be required reading for all peace-minded people. In one memorable passage, Taylor describes a conversation with a young Indian doctor, who complained that his training in Western medicine had made it impossible for him to serve his own people. India, he said, was too poor to afford Western medicine. Well, black America is not as poor or as undeveloped as India, but it is, on the whole, much too poor to afford the kind of medicine that most of white America is coming to take for granted. What it needs is the kind of doctors who served white America before doctors became $35,000-a-year-men—general practitioners who will make house calls and won't charge the moon for doing it.

Most of black America lives in a slum, be it rural or urban. Who will make these slums decent places to live in? White America clearly won't pay for it, and black America can't afford to pay white America to do it. Blacks, like the citizens of all poor and undeveloped nations, need to learn to do things—build buildings, run businesses and banks, educate and train themselves and their children—without spending much money. Will they, can they learn these things in white America's schools, even if they can get into the schools? It seems hardly likely. What is more likely is that they will be Higher Horizonized into wanting a house in the suburbs, which nobody will let them buy, or, if they are able to buy it, that they will leave the rest of their people behind, as isolated and leaderless as ever. In short, we can expect white schools to train some black émigrés, but not many effective black leaders.

[I have come to believe, perhaps because I must believe, that integration, of our schools or communities, is not a necessary condition of ending racism in our society. I must believe it, because it is clear to me, as to many others, that integration is no longer a possible or useful or in the short run even a desirable objective. The blacks, and for the most obvious and sensible reasons, no longer want it; the whites, by an almost overwhelming majority, will not tolerate it, and indeed would commit almost any crime to prevent it.

What we must work for is something quite different. The once perhaps noble ideal of the Melting Pot has grown into what Taylor, in *Richer By Asia*, though in a world-wide context, called "cultural imperialism." He quite rightly pointed out that the West could not have peace in the world unless and until it rid itself of cultural imperialism, and could live with many and widely different cultures in mutual tolerance and respect. This has now become the price of peace, liberty, and justice—even of the right-wingers' beloved law-and-order in the United States. There is no use any longer in talking about the American Way of Life—that way has excluded too many for too long. It is time to think of American *Ways of Life*, of sharply separated and perhaps widely different cultures existing in this country in mutual respect and under the equal protection of the law. Whether these cultures will someday merge and blend into one I cannot tell. I do not expect to see it in my lifetime, and I'm not even sure that I think it would be a good thing. In any case, the question is beside the point. Merely to create this poly-cultural society, to build into law and custom a respect for black and many other cultures and styles of life, will keep us busy for a long time.

I think it is as true as ever that black people who want to send their children to school with white children should be able to do so, and that white society should defend their right to do so. But it seems even more important that the vast majority of black people, whose children will for a long time be going to residentially segregated schools, should be able to control and run those schools. Since we have decided, by overwhelming majorities, not to let black people into our white America, and shut them off in a country of their own, it is only simple justice to stop exploiting that country, our colony of three hundred years, and let them develop it according to their own needs and wants.]

Work and Leisure

I speak here of work as most men know it: what you do to get money. About the future of work, two things seem clear. There is likely to be less and less of it; what there is, is likely to seem less and less like work. Men used to justify their lives by their work; the proof that they were useful was, first, that they were used, that someone found it worthwhile to pay them to do work, and secondly, in the work that they did. Today, more and more men are finding it impossible to get anyone to pay them to do anything. Of those who do work, a great many find in their work little or no cause for self-respect; if they didn't need the money, they wouldn't be doing it. The machine operator is becoming a machine tender. A skilled worker used to use machines, a complicated tool, to do what he wanted. Now, more and more, he merely feeds a machine, gives it what it needs, does what it wants. Mechanical baby-sitting. Give it its bottle and call me if it cries. W. H. Ferry recently said aptly that the model for much future work will be the now lowly night watchman. Men will tend more and more complicated machines: the proof that the job is going right will be that nothing is happening; only on the rare occasion when something goes wrong will they have something to do; usually it will be someone else's job to make sure that something doesn't go wrong again. Not much fun or satisfaction in this. [Driving by a big automobile assembly plant the other day, I was told by a young man who had worked there that about 80 percent of the workmen in the plant customarily used amphetamines so as to be able to stand the boredom of their jobs.]

We can expect this to become more so, not less. If so, more and more people will face two problems: how to justify, make meaningful their own lives, and how to fill up their time. The answer in both cases is to do something that seems very much worth doing. An important part of the business of education will be the finding of that something. Schools, therefore, must be places where children—and adults—may have time and opportunity to *do* a great many things, so as to find out which seem most worth doing. I emphasize the *do*. Very little of a child's time in school today is spent in *doing* anything; most of the time he is, or is supposed to be, either taking in information or, to prove that he has taken it in, spewing it back out. Sprinkled around here and there may be a tiny bit of art, or crafts, or sport, or drama, or music, or dance, but very few children are given enough time, *in school*, to work seriously on any of these things. If they do work seriously on them, it is outside of school, and their parents usually have to pay. Most of the children whose parents can't afford to pay, or whose communities can't or don't support special institutions outside the school system, get none of this. Thus we leave a huge vacuum in the minds and spirits of most children, and create a splendid market for mass entertainers and sensation peddlers of all kinds. So far it has worked, after a fashion; we have gotten by. In the long run, it won't do. The kinds of serious extracurricular interest that now occupy, and fill, and make worth living, the lives of a minority of people, will have to be found and enjoyed by all.

I don't want to suggest that these activities are limited to the ones I have suggested. Many people could and would, with great satisfaction, spend most of their time beautifying not just their own property, but any part of the environment they could reach, planting and tending flowers, shrubs, trees. I still think with great pleasure of some trees I planted once for my sister around a house where she lived only a year. I see those trees perhaps once a year. Even if I never saw them again, I would count well spent the time and backbreaking labor of planting them. I know they are there, and in a land short of trees.

I tend, however, to favor the arts, both plastic and performing, and crafts, not just because I like them, but because I suspect they have more room for thought, effort, care, discipline, and growth. They are not wells that one can drink dry. One will not get tired of them quickly, as one might get tired of, say, bowling if one were to do it for eight hours a day, five days a week. But there are other and quite different satisfactions. Hard physical labor can be immediately satisfying, if the work is done because it is worth doing and not just to put money in someone's pocket.

The point about these activities, this unpaid, for-its-own-sake work, is that it must call on and use a large part of the energies and talents of the worker. Bigger and better hobbies won't make a life. There must be an element of challenge, of striving for perfection, or at least improvement. A man can buy himself some power tools and spend five or six happy hours every week making bookshelves and turning pieces of driftwood into lamps. This is fine, as long as his main business is elsewhere. For thirty, or forty, or fifty hours a week it isn't enough, it won't do. He will have to begin to think of making objects of real beauty, of striving, like every artist, for a perfection that he can never quite reach. Otherwise he will get bored, and the power tools, like many today, will rust in the basement.

There are also a great many ways in which people can work to help other people. We may be wise and generous enough to do away with poverty, but we will still have plenty of people needing help—the sick, maimed, handicapped, very old, mentally disturbed. Not many people, certainly not enough people, will be interested in doing this kind of work, if we run our schools on the principle that the business of everyone in life is to get ahead—whatever that may mean—of everybody else. In short, the schools must become communities in which children learn, not by being preached at, but by living and doing it, to become aware and considerate of the needs of other people. It is not a question of setting up phony model legislatures, but of making the school a place in which a child has so much respect for his own work that he will respect the work of others, and will be naturally concerned to make the school a place where everyone can do best whatever kind of work he wants to do.

Poverty, Waste, and the Environment

These problems are so interconnected, not just with each other but with all the other problems discussed here, that it is hard to disconnect them enough to talk about them. The greed that threatens our environment also bars the way to an effective attack against poverty. Someone wrote to a magazine the other day about an article on the guaranteed national income, asking furiously, "Why should I give up some of my hard earned money to help support some bum who won't work?" The question is beyond rational argument. If that's the way you feel about other people, then that's the way you're going to think. Similarly, there must be many lumber barons who, hearing conservationists say that redwoods that have lived for thousands of years should be saved for posterity, say irritably to themselves—though not to the public, for whom smooth lies are cooked up—"What the hell has posterity ever done for me?" What indeed? There is no good answer to the question. What we need is more of the kind of people who would never ask it, who feel themselves a living link in a chain of humanity. What we need is people who really love their country—not just hate whomever its government calls its enemies—

and who will show their love for it, as a starter, by not covering it with garbage, junk, and beer cans.

We know something about greed, not much but a little. The greedy man is a man who is trying to fill up a hole inside himself, to make up with wealth, position, esteem, and power for his lost or never developed sense of his own worth. The greedy man is also likely to be a vengeful one, always trying and failing to score off someone, or the whole world, for some past injury or wrong. The lumber baron who strips a hillside of redwoods, the steel magnate who destroys the dunes at the foot of Lake Michigan to make room for a new steel mill, the company manager who fills the air or the waters around him with poison, and the tourist who throws a beer can and a paper bag full of garbage out his car window, are all alike in one important respect: in some part of their minds they are all saying, "There, you bastards!" Their lives are a kind of war that they can never win or end, because they don't know what it is they are lacking, or where or how to find it. They can never have enough; the hole inside can never be filled. The problem of education is to help children grow up without these unfillable holes, this relentless need to eat up the whole earth. It's not a question of doing away with greed, some of which is natural, but of having some kind of reasonable limit to it. L. L. Bean, owner of a renowned Maine sporting goods store, is reported to have once said, when someone told him that with a little effort he could triple his business, "What for? I can't eat four meals a day." Just so; enough is enough.

Freedom

Not long ago I spoke to a PTA meeting at a very good elementary school. As always, I urged that children be given greater freedom to decide what they should learn and how they should learn it. One parent came up to me after the meeting and said, "It seems to me that what we have to do is give children gradually less and less freedom as they grow up, so as to get them ready for what adult life will be like." Many people have said such things to me, at one time or another. It is hard to know how to reply. What can you say to someone who tells you, in this supposedly free country, that there is no real freedom for most people, that this condition is not bad, or at least cannot be changed, and that the best we can do for our children is help them get used to it?

There seems to be no scientific way to prove that freedom is a good thing, a value worth preserving. I believe that it is, maybe just because, in the words of W. H. Ferry, I like to "feel free." I also believe that freedom is in serious danger in this country, precisely because so many people, like the parent I spoke of, do not feel free, never did, don't expect to, and hence don't know what freedom is, or why it should be worth making such a fuss about. For a great many Americans, freedom is little more than a slogan that makes it seem right to despise, hate, and even kill any foreigner who supposedly has less of it than they do. When, rather rarely, they meet someone who feels free and acts free and takes his freedom seriously, they are more likely than not to get frightened or angry. "What are you, some kind of a nut?" For alas, the man who has no real freedom, or thinks he hasn't, doesn't think about how to get it: he thinks about how to take it away from those who do have it.

Whatever makes men feel less free, even if it does not take away any particular right or liberty, lessens and threatens the freedom of all of us. What sorts of things make a man feel unfree? One is being pushed around: having to submit to other men whom he cannot reach, see, or talk to, and over whom he feels he has no control. Another is not knowing what goes on, feeling that he is not told, and cannot find, the truth. Still another is feeling that he has no real say about his own life, no real choices to make; that the decisions that determine whether he goes this way or that are made by other men, behind his back. The great danger to freedom in this society lies in the fact that the objective conditions that make men feel this way are increasing and are sure to continue to increase.

There are two reasons for this. One is that the organizations with which we have to deal in various aspects of our lives—business, government agencies—are growing bigger. The other is that, as if obeying some kind of law of organizations, they are growing more centralized, more depersonalized, more bureaucratic. The first time a problem comes up before an organization—and to any organization we outsiders are all and always problems—some one person considers it and tries to solve it. But, doing so, he sets a precedent; the precedent soon turns into a system, the system into a rule. Before long, the only people the organization will allow us to talk to are employees as helpless, as powerless to make decisions, as ourselves: "I'm sorry, that's the rule: what can I do, I only work here?"

Once in a while, with luck and persistence, one can fight one's way far enough into the machine to find someone who can and will decide and act. Some years ago I ordered some goods from a leading local department store. The store told me that they could fill only half my order, which they sent me. They then had the nerve to send me a bill for the full amount of the order, saying that I could have a credit for that part of it they could not fill. I refused to pay the bill, saying that I wanted all of what I had ordered, and would pay for it when I got it. Then came a stream of form letters, at first peremptory, then threatening, full of talk about attorneys and going to my bank. I wrote indignant and angry letters in return. After about six months, a letter came that was actually signed by a human being. I quickly called him up on the phone, told him the story; he apologized and said he would see what he could do; within a few weeks the rest of the order had arrived, and I paid the bill. Happy ending. But it wouldn't have been so happy if the store had had my money. And the average man hasn't the time to write a dozen letters to a store and doesn't feel free enough to thumb his nose at all this talk about attorneys and banks.

The government often seems just as remote. I have written many letters to the President, the Vice President, Cabinet members, or Congressmen. Once in a while a Congressman will answer my letter in a way that suggests that he has read it. Most of the time what comes back is form letters and mimeographed handouts. Doubtless somebody reads every letter, but it is rarely anyone who can do anything, or even who cares what I think, beyond perhaps occasionally adding my letter to a kind of tally. The business of these letter-readers is not to carry my thoughts and wishes to their superiors, but to stand between me and them, to mollify me, to persuade me to go away, stop bothering them, let them get on with what they think is *their* business. And, I should add, to accept as true whatever story they have decided to tell me. For our government grows not only bigger, but steadily more secret and less truthful. It does not even try to hide its secrecy and untruthfulness: high officials tell us with increasing bluntness that in many areas we have no right to know what is going on, and that they aren't going to tell us.

Another threat to our sense of our own freedom lies in the attacks that men increasingly make on our own privacy. These are of two kinds, unauthorized eavesdropping and what might be called authorized or compulsory eavesdropping. About the former, little needs to be said; there have been many articles during the past year about the extraordinary wire-tapping and eavesdropping devices that have been developed and are being increasingly used. A few libertarians are indignant, a few voices are raised in Washington, but little will be changed. There will be more eavesdropping rather than less: many departments of our federal, state, and local governments, and a growing number of private agencies, will continue to break the laws; the average man will accept, more and more, perhaps willingly, perhaps not, the idea that the authorities can and will listen to his conversations any time they feel like it.

By compulsory eavesdropping I mean the kind of so-called psychological or personality testing that requires people to answer questions about themselves—their thoughts, wishes, dreams, fears—that they would ordinarily rather not answer. To get a great many jobs, you must take such tests. Though scorn is rightly heaped on them, they are likely to grow rather than shrink; they make money, and they pander not only to the current love of prying into other people's lives but also to the current superstition that "science" can somehow do away with the risks in human affairs. I also mean the kind of information-gathering now done under the name of security making people testify under oath about their past beliefs, associations, etc.; or collecting such information about them from other people—friends, landlords, neighbors. There is talk of gathering together all such information that various snoopers have gathered about citizens of this country, and putting it into one great combined gossip file somewhere in Washington. The freedom-loving minority will protest, but the chances are that this gossip gathering will increase rather than decrease. To that extent, the average citizen will continue to feel less and less free.

How are we to save and extend freedom in the face of these pressures? Obviously, we need a generation—many generations—whose sense and love of their own freedom is strong, much stronger than our own. We are not getting them from our schools today. Polls taken of high-school students show, first, that they know very little about the Bill of Rights, and secondly, that much of what they do know, or are told, they don't believe in. On one poll, something over 40 percent of those questioned said that police should be able to use the third degree—that is, torture—on people suspected of crime. Their other replies were no less authoritarian and frightening.

With our schools as they are, this is not surprising. What is most shocking and horrifying about public education today is that in almost all schools the children are treated, most of the time, like convicts in jail. Like black men in South Africa, they cannot move without written permission, and the buildings are full of monitors—that is, spies and police, most of them students themselves—to make sure that they have this permission. During a large part of the day, they cannot even speak without permission. And yet, on second thought, this is not what shocks me most. What shocks me most is that the students do not resist this, do not complain about it, do not mind it, even defend it as being necessary and for their own good. They have truly been made ready for slavery.

An assistant superintendent of a big city public school system once gave a talk to about sixty or seventy high-school students, most of them blacks, and a group of teachers, myself among them. His message was this: You'd better be good in school and do what the teacher tells you, always, right away quick, with no questions or argument or back talk. Why? Because for every one of you students the school keeps a little card, and on that card every teacher you have can write down anything and everything that you do that he or she doesn't like, and when you get out of school and start looking for a job, that little card will go to your prospective employer, and so on through most or all of your working life. I was horrified; I could hardly believe my ears. He went on to talk about some of the positive side of school—careers, job opportunities, the usual antidropout pep talk. As he spoke, a voice in my head was clamoring questions. Is this really true? Is this common? Do the students ever find out what goes on their card? Do they ever get a chance to give their side of the story? Is there any chance for appeal? Are there, in fact, any of the protections our law customarily gives to adults, accused of crime and threatened with punishment?

When the question period came I waited, expectantly, for students to ask these questions. It was their meeting; they were the victims of these abuses: let them speak first. But none did. Finally, barely able to control my indignation, I asked them myself. The speaker was very cool. He did not know about other cities; this was the general practice in his city. No, the students did not know what they were accused of nor, if they did, did they have any chance to defend themselves. Yes, it might result in injustice here and there—what made all this hardest for me to believe and understand was that the speaker was himself a black man—but on the whole it seemed a sensible way to run things. In any case it was the system; his business wasn't to change it, or complain about it; he was doing more than most men in his position in even telling the students about it. Which I guess was true.

Later, in classes, we discussed the matter further. Some students had already known about these cards; those who had not known were not surprised—it was about what they had expected. They were utterly unable to understand what it was about this business that got me so upset. I asked them about hall passes. Oh yes, they all had to fill them out. What did they think about not being able to move without written permission? They didn't mind. One boy, intelligent, who thought of himself as liberal or even radical and was active in the peace and civil-rights movements, said, "They have to run the school like that, otherwise the kids would tear the building down." I said, "You mean you think you would?" He said. "No, but the others would. If they could move around when they wanted, they'd abuse the privilege." The privilege! He might have been a convict talking about his daily hour of exercise in the prison yard.

Last fall a girl I know, who had just gone into junior high school, brought home a mimeographed pamphlet, "Welcome to XYZ Junior High," which had been given to all students. I read it. It was an extraordinary document. I couldn't help comparing it with a pamphlet that the Army put out for its new recruits. From the two pamphlets, the Army seemed about a hundred times more friendly, welcoming, and pleasant than the XYZ Junior High School. The Army's message was, "We're glad you're here; there's a lot of interesting things going on in this outfit; we think you'll like it and get along fine." The Junior High School's message was, "We're watching you; we're on to your tricks; just step out of line for one second and see how long it takes for the roof to fall in on you." It could have served as a model for the regulations of a maximum-security prison run for exceptionally dangerous offenders.

What is the effect of this kind of treatment on children? Just what one might expect. It destroys most of their sense of their own worth, if they have any; if they don't, it makes it almost impossible for them to get any. It convinces them that they, and certainly almost everyone else, are not fit for responsibility or worthy of respect and trust. By denying them the chance to have, and use, and enjoy, and value their own freedom, it persuades them, or makes them easy to persuade, that true personal freedom is at least valueless and at most dangerous. In short, it is splendid training for slavery. If we want a country in which everyone has his place, slave to everyone above him, master to everyone below him; a country in which respect for and obedience to authority is the guiding rule of life; a country, in short, like Germany in the generation before Hitler—if this is what we want, we are on the right track. On the right track, and picking up speed; Edgar Friedenburg, perhaps the only writer to point out (in *The Vanishing Adolescent and Coming of Age in America*) that schools consistently and deliberately violate the civil liberties of their students, has recently written that our schools are seeing a rapid increase in violent corporal punishment—not just knuckle-rapping, but prolonged and severe beatings. As they say, it figures.

On the other hand, if we want a country in which people will resist the growing pressures to conformity and servility and will vigorously defend their own rights and the rights of others, then we had better begin to give children some real freedom in school—freedom to move, to talk, to plan and use their time, to direct and assess their own learning, to act, and be treated, like sensible human beings.

—1968

BLACKBOARD BUNGLE

Learning to Teach in Urban Schools, by Dorothy M. McGeoch with Carol R. Bloomgarden. Ellen O. Furedi, Lynne W. Randolph and Eugene D. Ruth, Jr.

This is a well-made, interesting and revealing little book. Unlike many books about education, it is clear, concise, and candid. It is also very sad.

It is the story, told in their own words, of four young teachers' five years of teaching in city slum schools. These young people are appealing. They are earnest, determined, enthusiastic, eager to help the children they teach, unsparing in their criticism of themselves, ready to take advice and criticism from any quarter. One can't help feeling that we are lucky to have such people going into teaching. Surely, with such to work with, we will be able before long to solve the terrible educational problems of our urban slums.

This is what makes the book sad. For these people, for all their fine qualities of mind and character, and for all the ingenuity, energy, and dedication they bring to their work, are almost certain, like most other teachers, to wind up doing far more harm than good. In spite of all they have read and been told about slum children, they are hopelessly miseducated, almost wholly unprepared for the experience before them, almost wholly incapable of learning from it. They do not understand, any more than did their own teachers, the real nature of learning. They do not know how school looks to children, how these children think and feel and react, why they behave as they do. They have no idea of the ways in which children's feelings about their environment affect their learning, nor of the kind of environment that might make learning possible, or even likely, nor of how to create such an environment in their own classes. Far from knowing the answers to such questions, they never even thought to ask them.

There is that old story about a countryman who, asked the way to the post office, tried several times to give directions and then said, "Well, the fact is, you can't get to the post office from here." From where these young people are starting, they can't get to where they want to go, and where we want them to go—to an education that will really enrich and illuminate the lives of their students. Their model of what they are trying to do is so fundamentally and radically wrong that no amount of patching and tinkering will make it work.

Hear them talk about their teaching:

> TEACHER A: I would be nervous coming to school in the morning. That's why I started out tough in my own classroom.... All last summer I dreaded it.... I looked forward to teaching with fear and trembling...I was really very scared of it all, but it was much smoother than I expected. I had anticipated all kinds of things going wrong, children not doing what I told them, and complete chaos. I do believe that things have to be orderly or the children are not going to learn.... I don't mind when they whisper or talk quietly about what they have to do, but even that should be kept to a minimum.

This, let me note, of children whose greatest handicap is that they lack experience in the use of language. To continue:

> TEACHER B: The gym teacher helped me to get organized. We did the same thing every week. The boys threw basketballs and the girls jumped rope. I had thought we might have races and team games, but it didn't work because I couldn't set up a new routine each week.

> TEACHER C: Sometimes I ask another teacher where she is in the book. If she's as slow as I am,

I feel good. And if I find someone who is four-teen chapters ahead, I feel sick to my stomach...

The class feels that it is a disgrace to be behind. They realize that there is a schedule to be met, and other people are meeting it and they're not.

I finally achieved an orderly entrance to assembly that way.... I was determined to get order.

TEACHER D: I felt—and I have continued to feel—that good discipline is a matter of demanding and receiving attention when you want it.... It will be very hard to acquire a good, firm grip on the class again.

In order to establish discipline in a class *so that eventually you will be able to teach* [italics added], you have to set up routines and everlast-ingly enforce them.

THE EDITOR: "Every beginning teacher worries about discipline. There is but one thought in the minds of most neophyte teachers: "Will the chil-dren obey me?""

These quotes can only begin to suggest these teachers' panicky obsession with order, control, obedience, discipline. Their model of education and the classroom is an assembly line in a factory. Down the line come the children, a row of empty lugs; beside the line, each in his place, stand the teachers, pouring into these lugs out of contain-ers marked English, math, etc., prescribed quantities of knowledge. The pouring is easy—anyone can do that; anyone can do the things they tell you to do in the teachers' manuals. The real problem, the teacher's real job, is to get children to sit still on the conveyor belt while he does the pouring. This is why these teachers, like almost all teachers, think that learning is a by-product of order, that if you can just create the order, the learning must follow.

The system seems to work in the suburbs. Why doesn't it work in the slums?

Sociologists make learned theories about cultural deprivation. This has something to do with it, but not much. Even in the suburbs, school is unspeakably dull, and usually painful, but the middle-class child puts up with it, because his elders dangle a carrot in front of him and wave a stick behind him, and he wants the carrot and fears the stick. The slum child, and indeed the failing child in any school, after a while no longer believes in the carrot and no longer fears the stick. You aren't going to get those prizes they dangle in front of you. As for punishments, well, if you're a child, there is only so much that society can do to you, and you soon get used to that. Not only used—even proud of it; when a child has been, so to speak, ritually cast out of society a certain number of times, he soon feels that he would rather be outside than inside.

For the slums, we need something better. Any order we get is going to have to be a by-product of real learning, learning that satisfies the curiosity of the children, that helps them to make some sense of their lives and the world they live in, that helps make these lives, if not pleasant, at least bearable.

How can we get such learning in the classroom? Some good work has been done on this, and some good books written on it—like Sylvia Ashton-Warner's *Teacher* and Paul Goodman's *Compulsory Miseducation;* unfortunately, neither of these books is on the four young teachers' reading list. So, barring a miracle, they will go on struggling to make their classrooms into learning factories, until they give up teaching, or get cynical, or decide to teach "able"—which means docile—pupils, or go into administration. What a waste of their talent and idealism.

—1965

CHILDREN IN PRISON

Village School Downtown, by Peter Schrag.
Death at an Early Age: The Destruction of the Hearts and Minds of Negro Children in the Boston Public Schools, by Jonathan Kozol.

One of the most striking and painful social events of our time has been what can only be called the downfall of our big city schools. It has helped drive out of the city millions of people whose wealth, training, talent, and interests might otherwise have helped to make or keep our cities civilized and satisfying places. At the same time, it has increasingly alienated from the city and its institutions and culture more and more of those people whom poverty and/or color oblige to remain there. The schools claim, with some reason, that they are among the victims rather than the causes of urban decay, but the fact is that, despite their always difficult problems and often good intentions, they are at least as much cause as victim.

How bad are our city schools? How did they get so bad? For answer, these two books lift the lid off the schools of one city, my own city of Boston. They do so in very different ways. Schrag's is an outsider's view of the whole school system—thorough, inclusive, well researched, and as objective as a deeply concerned educator could make it. It is also witty, perceptive, and fair. Kozol's book, on the other hand, is an insider's wholly personal cry of outrage and pain at the things he saw done to black children in the schools where he taught. He is in no sense objective; though truthful, he is hardly even fair. He is not concerned, as is Schrag, to give the devil his due, but only to show what the devil is doing.

From Schrag we learn, first of all, that:

More than a third of the city's schools are over fifty years old; several are now into their second century, while eighteen of the twenty schools that are more than ninety percent Negro were built before World War I. Dilapidated structures, some of them overcrowded and ill-used, litter the older neighborhoods. Nevertheless, "For two years the city has not built a single new school, even though $29 million in construction funds has been approved by the Mayor and city council." The equipment is no better than the buildings:

In some (schools), teachers try to conduct classes jammed with forty-five children; in others they must operate in the basement or in temporary converted auditoriums and lunchrooms. Few of the junior high schools have libraries, and the elementary schools have none. Many of the texts are outdated, torn, dirty, and often, when they are modern, there are not enough to go around.

What is most to the point is that neither the administrators nor the elected School Committee seems concerned about the problem, or even willing to admit that there is a problem. Thus, Schrag tells us, "In Pittsburgh, the administration publishes pictures of obsolete buildings in an effort to rally public support for new construction, fliers are issued describing the inadequacies of the system.... But not in Boston. Instead of calling administrators to task for their failures, the School Committee colludes with them to obscure and deny...." Of course, in a pinch, first-rate education can be given in second-rate buildings. But the Boston School system is not in a pinch, and does not even claim to be.

The system is inbred:

The majority of the city's teachers share similar lower middle-class backgrounds, attended the same public or parochial schools, and graduated from the same colleges.... Among the teachers are a few Italians and Jews, a handful of Negroes—about one teacher in two hundred is a Negro—and even one or two Jewish principals [Boston's first black principal was named in the fall of 1966]. But...all but one member of the Board of Superintendents, the senior staff of the system, are graduates of Boston College, all have risen through the ranks and have been in the system for more than three decades, all are well over fifty years old, all are Catholics, and all, excepting Superintendent William H. Ohrenberger...are Irishmen.

Schrag quotes a leading Catholic critic of the system as saying that to succeed in Boston "you have to be a Catholic—it would be unthinkable to hire a non-Catholic as superintendent. This is a closed system. They never go outside and they never let outsiders in."

The kind of learning to which this system and these people are dedicated is, as might be expected, one based almost wholly on the rote-learning of disconnected and outdated facts. The teachers themselves are picked according to their ability to spit up such facts on competitive exams, and they carry the method into their own classes. Perhaps the grimmest part of Schrag's book is his verbatim quotations of what actually happens in Boston classrooms. The teacher in an English class discussing the poem "I Have a Rendezvous with Death," asks "Now, what does rendezvous mean?"

A. (The boy stands up, as required.) It means a meeting.
Q. When does this take place?
A. In the Spring.
Q. How does he treat death in these lines?
A. Like a person.
Q. What do you call that?
A. Personification.

and so on. In another class we have:

Q. What is Italy good for as far as Napoleon is concerned?

A. It's a place where he can put his relatives in
   office.
Q. He is a good family man. What did he get in
   Italy?
A. Art works.

In another,

Q. Did we win the Revolution, Foote?
A. Yes.
Q. Of course we did.... So then we had to establish
   a plan of government that was called what?
A. The Constitution.
Q. I'll hit you in the head. (Hands are up)
A. The Articles of Confederation.
Q. What were they? (Pages flip in the textbook)
A. Our first plan of government.

and so on. In still another:

Q. Why would they go by dog sled?
A. Because there's a lot of snow.
Q. What's the land like along the coast, Michael?
A. Mountains.
Q. What do they do on the coast?
A. Hunt?
Q. What do they do on any coast?
A. Fish.

What is astonishing about these classes is that though one is a
fifth grade class, one a seventh, one a ninth, and one an advanced
placement class for seniors, one can hardly tell, from the quality of the
discussion, which one is which. In none of them is the discussion as
lively, fluent, or interesting as, in better schools, one might hear even
in the first grade.

The result of this kind of education is what one might expect.
Boston once led the nation in the percentage of its students that finished high school, and that gained admission to leading colleges. Now
only about a fourth of its high school graduates go to college at all,

and Schrag's figures—4,454 high school graduates in a school population of 93,000—suggest that a good many of those students who enter high school do not finish. Achievement test scores (for whatever little they are worth) at all grade levels are well below national norms, and grow further behind as the grades advance.

Why did this once workable system—it cannot be said ever to have had very much imagination—lose so much of its energy, conviction, and morale? Schrag is not explicit here, but he hints that the schools began to decline when the old-time Yankees in the system were replaced by Irish Catholics. This diagnosis is too simple and too particular. In the first place, some of the boldest and most imaginative innovators in education today are Catholics, so that it does not necessarily follow that a school system run and dominated by Catholics must produce bad education. In the second place, the decline of the Boston schools has been paralleled, if not quite matched, by other school systems in which Catholic influence, Irish or otherwise, was much less strong or not strong at all.

What seems to me most true in Schrag's diagnosis, not only in Boston but everywhere, is that the teachers who took over the schools—in Boston, from the old Yankees; in other cities, from other people—came from predominantly nonintellectual or even antiintellectual lower middle-class backgrounds, and that they looked on education very much as another branch of the civil service. You didn't go into teaching because you loved learning or believed in its importance, because education meant anything to you or had done anything for you, or because there was anything you particularly wanted to teach, but because the schools were one place that a person without much in the way of ability, training, or connections *could* get in and, once in, could be sure, if he kept his nose clean and did what he was told, of staying in, until he retired with his pension. In other words, you went into education for the same reason that others went into the police or the Post Office or other parts of the civil service— because it was a safe, secure, and respectable way to move up a rung or two from the bottom of the socio-economic ladder.

Such people, going into teaching for such reasons, are likely, whatever their ethnic or religious backgrounds, to be poor teachers, and poorest of all for the children of our city slums. For one thing, they are generally uneasy about their own status, and consequently prone to overrate the importance of authority and control in the classroom, see challenges to their position and authority where none are meant, and turn every personal difference or difficulty into such a challenge. For another—Edgar Friedenberg has written often and well about this—they are likely to be bourgeois or commercial in their own values and attitudes, and thus both profoundly hostile to and threatened by the more aristocratic and anarchic values and attitudes of children, above all slum children. For another, they are likely to be neither very interested nor very interesting. They see education only as a way of "getting ahead," and since they have not got very far ahead they are not very persuasive. To their unspoken or spoken advice, "Study hard, and you can be like me," their students answer silently (and not always silently), "You creep, who wants to be like you?" Finally, their recent escape from poverty tends to make them particularly contemptuous, fearful, and hostile toward those who are still poor—feelings they are not skillful enough to conceal even if they happen to wish to.

The job itself takes its toll. I have done all my teaching in exceptionally favorable circumstances—using materials and methods of my own inventing or choosing, working with relatively small classes made up of children who, if not eager, were at least docile, and under administrators who, even when they could not give me understanding or support, at least gave me some freedom and respect. Even then, and although I am deeply interested in education and very much enjoy the company of almost all children, even then teaching has often been for me a difficult, demanding, often heartbreakingly discouraging job. For someone to whom it is only a job, not a calling, obliged most of the time to do exactly what he is told, forbidden, even if he wanted, to use more than a tiny part of his initiative or intelligence or imagination, compelled to play in his classes only the roles of taskmaster, policeman, and judge, harassed and hampered with an infinity of paperwork and petty administrative duties, faced with large classes of bored or hostile children, neither well paid nor highly esteemed by society or even his own "profession," in which he is all too often looked on and treated like the lowest factory laborer or foot-soldier—for such a person, teaching must be, at best, drudgery and, at worst, a nightmare. A man I met only last summer, after hearing some talk about educational innovation, said to me, "I'm afraid you younger fellows are going to have to do that stuff—I'm forty years old, and I'm burned out." For a second I was surprised; but not when I found out that, during his entire working life, to support his family he had had to do two full-time jobs, teaching and one other, every day.

Such men, in their own way, are a kind of hero, and we must respect them, if for no other reason than that they keep going. We must also ask ourselves, as we rightly deplore the rigidity, narrowness, and authoritarianism of most schools, what freedom means or possibly could mean to such people, who feel that they do not have it and never have had it. To be sure, many of them are ready to argue, fight, and even die (and perhaps kill everyone else) in defense of "Freedom"; but this means only that they fear that in any other country they would be driven even harder and rewarded even less. If they must be slaves, this is the best place to be one.

It is asking too much to expect such men and women to see, let alone understand, freedom as a value to be nourished and protected and fought for. They can only see it, at best, as a luxury, one they have never been able to afford; and it is not surprising that they should resent those people, including children, who seem to be able, or act as if they were able, to afford it. At worst, they see it as a positive danger, something that can only get a man in trouble. Hardly a day ago, a teacher said to me, "Society stamps us into a mold as soon as we grow up"—here he made a sort of egg-crate stamping motion with his hands—"and it rejects whoever doesn't fit. What's going to happen to kids educated your way? How are they going to survive?" In much this vein, someone once wrote, "Swift death awaits the cow who leads a revolt against milking." Such is the worldview of all too many teachers. Be quiet. Do what you're told. Don't kick over the pail.

It is only natural that many of these people should have developed a bad case of what Edmond Taylor, in his excellent book *Richer By Asia*, called the sahib-sickness—a conviction that the people you once set out to help cannot be helped and are in fact not worth helping—and that the many frustrations and resentments teachers feel in their work and their lives should eventually turn into an active contempt and hatred of the children they are supposedly trying to teach.

In his book Jonathan Kozol shows how far this hatred has gone, and to what dreadful consequences it has led. It is an account of things he saw, heard, said, and did in a year's worth of substitute teaching in a number of Roxbury schools. He has changed names and places, to make it impossible to identify any particular teacher or school. Otherwise, the tale he tells us is true.

It is a tale of unrelieved, and almost unbelievable, callousness and cruelty. The principal victim in his book—by no means the only one—is a black boy named Stephen, "eight years old...tiny, desperate, unwell...an indescribably mild and unmalicious child...a ward of the State of Massachusetts [who] often comes into school badly beaten." The insults and violence heaped on this helpless, harmless little child almost defy description. He likes to draw, and draws imaginatively and well, but the Art teacher, who prefers mimeographed designs neatly colored in, screams at him when she sees his work—mind you, he is eight—"Give me that! Your paints are all muddy! You've made it a mess! Look at what he's done! He's mixed up the colors! I don't know why we waste good paper on this child!...Garbage! Junk! And garbage is one thing I will not have." Though Stephen's teachers knew, and often said, that he was not in his right mind, he was frequently beaten on the hand with a rattan—a long, flexible, painful bamboo stick. Kozol estimates, "It happened for a while as often as once every month and probably more often, probably closer to once or twice a week." Another child was beaten on a hand with an infected finger: the infection was so badly aggravated that he had to spend several days in the hospital. When the child's mother complained to the responsible authorities at school, she was told that the whipping had been "done right"; the only other response made by these same authorities was to send the child a Get Well card in the hospital.

It is grotesque: it sounds made up. Here are teachers talking about the way to use the rattan on children: "When you do it, you want to snap it abruptly or else you are not going to get the kind of effect you want." "Leave it overnight in vinegar or water if you want it to really sting the hands." When Kozol asked a teacher whether this kind of beating was against the law, he was told, "Don't worry about the law. You just make damn sure that no one's watching." Another teacher advised him, when he whacked a kid, to do it when nobody was looking, and to make sure not to leave any bruise marks on him. Then you could just deny it coldly if it came to court. On another occasion, when two children claimed that their homework papers, which they said they had handed in, were lost—something that often happened in the endless shuffle of substitute teachers—they were called to the front of the room by the teacher and there told that they were lying. And so on, and on.

One asks oneself, "Are these horrors true? Have indignation and resentment made Kozol exaggerate or distort what really happened? Is he a credible witness?" There is no doubt that he is. The schools call him a troublemaker, but the charge is absurd. It is clear that he leaned over backwards, to what he himself admits was a shameful degree, to stay out of trouble with the authorities and to do what they wanted. Far from looking for an excuse to fight the system, he did all he could (and far more than he should) to avoid a fight. Who can forget the child standing for weeks on end at the door of his "classroom" and silently and futilely pleading to be allowed in? Anyway, I have heard enough black boys talking, not bitterly but jokingly, like old soldiers rehashing a tough campaign, about their own experiences in the Boston schools, the shouts, insults, cuffings, slammings against the walls, and canings, to feel sure that what Kozol tells us is the truth—though probably only a small part of it—and that, at least to black children, the Boston public schools are every bit as contemptuous, callous, and cruel as he says.

But he tells another kind of story that is in a way even more significant. These are stories about the things he was not allowed to do for or with black children, in many cases things that other teachers were allowed to do for the few white children in the same school. Thus the reading teacher gave one white child an expensive book, helped another to go to summer camp, invited a third and his parents to visit her. But when Kozol gave a black child a lift home, or took Stephen to the Peabody Museum, or visited his home, he was reprimanded. He was told not to let Stephen come near him in class, to discourage all the child's attempts to make him his desperately needed and only friend.

Still more important, every time he was able, in his teaching, to catch the interest and enthusiasm of the children, he was made to stop. Once he was forbidden to give the children some supplementary material he had prepared for history, which would make more clear to them the connection between the invention of the cotton gin and slavery. Once he was told to stop using a book called *Mary Jane*, about the first black in a Southern town to enter an all-white school, in spite of the fact that the children, even those considered bad readers, were reading it with enormous interest. He was not allowed to use a biography of Martin Luther King, Jr, which excited many children. He was severely criticized for giving the children a writing assignment in which, because they could truly describe the world as they saw it, they wrote expressively and well. He was not allowed to display, because they were supposedly too difficult, some paintings of Paul Klee, though the children found them fascinating. He was not allowed to read, although the children enjoyed them, poems by Yeats or Frost. And he was finally fired for reading a poem, Langston Hughes's "The Landlord," which many of the children liked so much that they memorized it.

The hard fact is that with few exceptions our city slum schools, like many of the broken-spirited children in them, have fallen back on the strategy of deliberate failure. They had a vested interest in that failure. They do not mean to succeed, or to let anyone else succeed. I have by now heard or read a good many stories by or about teachers in many cities who have succeeded in reaching and teaching slum children. In almost every case they have found themselves in constant difficulty with the authorities, and have usually, sooner or later, been fired. This is to be expected. The less our city schools are able to do, the harder they must cling to the excuse that nothing can be done, and the more deeply they must be threatened by anyone who by succeeding undermines the last shaky prop to their self-respect—the dogma that poor city children cannot be taught.

Through Kozol's voice, we hear the children calling for help. How are we to help? Here Schrag takes a position for which it is hard to find any sympathy. He describes some of the attempts to rescue the children that are now going on in Boston: Operation Exodus, in which black parents, at their own expense, bus their children to less crowded schools in white sections of the city; Metco, in which small numbers of black children are bused to white schools in certain suburbs; the Boardman School, where the school system has been willing to allow at least some experiment and innovation; and the New School for Children, a private school set up and run by blacks, many of them middle-class, and supported largely by outside money. All of these Schrag angrily dismisses, saying that by deflecting attention from the "real problem" and draining off anger, energy, and money that might be used to meet it, they may make the situation worse.

This is a typical way of looking at things in our time; we like big, top-down solutions to problems; we are all infected with the General Staff mentality. Here it must be challenged on several counts. In the first place, though Schrag doesn't mean it to be, it is callous, like telling people trying to rescue a drowning man from a lake that their efforts turn us away from the real problem—the need to drain the lake, so that no one could drown in it. Even if true, so what? In the second place, it ignores the obvious, that every time we find ways to educate black children, whether in private or special public schools in their own neighborhoods or in white schools outside them, we help destroy the myth that black children are uneducable, and thus make ever more clear that the responsibility for their failure to learn in most public schools lies not with them or their families, but with the schools. In the third place, the great gimmick to which Schrag seems to have pinned his hopes—the idea of a metropolitan educational district joining city and suburbs (which considered *in vacuo* may not be a bad idea)—is for the time being politically dead. A conference of national educational leaders discussed the matter in detail for many days in the summer of 1967. Their all but unanimous opinion was that in almost all of our major cities, with the possible exception of Pittsburgh, metropolitanism has virtually no chance. For one thing, and for obvious reasons, the suburbs are against it. The superintendent of a suburban system much admired by Schrag, and one which is taking in some black city children, said bluntly, "Our School Board is not going to agree to vote itself out of existence."

Precisely. The good boards will hold fast to their autonomy because they are good: the bad because they are bad. Nor is it easy to see why Schrag thinks the people of Boston, who voted in such numbers for Mrs. Hicks (onetime chairman of the School Committee, narrowly defeated for Mayor) because they see her as one of their own, will vote to merge their schools with the suburbs. It is easy to see with what arguments and with what effect Mrs. Hicks and others like her would oppose such a move.

Finally, blacks themselves are turning against the idea of metropolitanism, and, increasingly, even against the idea of school integration. They say, the hell with sending our children to schools where *the very best* that can happen to them is that the ruling white majority will be nice to them, maybe give them a crumb here and a crumb there. Many of them want schools run by black people for black people, and, as things are going, they may have a good chance of getting them. So good a chance, indeed, that some writers are beginning to suggest that if we get metropolitanism it will be for reasons that are anti-black rather than pro, that is, in order to prevent them from gaining any real and effective political or educational power.

For the time being, then, metropolitanism is irrelevant. Where then, and how, are the black children of Roxbury, and of black ghettos in big cities all over the country, to look for help? In three places, I think. First, if we stop heckling urban white people about integration, they may come slowly to realize that their schools are no damn good, for white children as well as black, and may then begin to consider how to make them better for all. [There are some encouraging signs, in Boston and other cities, that this is beginning to happen.] Here we must admire Schrag's courage, fairness, and common sense in saying that the Racial Imbalance Law in Massachusetts can be seen, as it is seen by many in Boston, as a demand by those rich enough to avoid having to mingle with blacks that those who are not rich mingle with them more closely than ever. The demand is unfair, and, what is more to the point, it cannot now be made to work. If white liberals want, as they should, to attack segregation, the place to attack it is in housing, *where they live*. Never mind how to get black children into the schools in lower middle-class Charlestown, South Boston, and the North End. Worry instead about how to get black adults, and their children, into the rich suburbs of Milton, Newton, or Wellesley. If we are to get, as eventually we must, integration in schools, this is now the way for white people to work for it.

Meanwhile, there is much that our city dwellers, with only the resources they now have, could do to make their schools better. By now many American educators have seen schools, in Leicestershire in Great Britain, that provide their average children of lower-income families with first-class education, in spite of many ill-designed and outdated buildings, low budgets, and forty children per class. We can learn much from them if we want to. Even in the conditions Kozol describes, some good things could be done. He writes, "The pupils who could read were insulted and bored by the kinds of books that filled the cupboards." Probably rightly so. But why not ask them to say why, and in what way, they were bored and insulted, and from that point to consider in general what makes books good or bad? If the textbooks in the schools are out of date, why not compare them with up-to-date information—not hard nor expensive to get—to see how the world has changed since the texts were printed? If the schools have no good books, why not go to second-hand paperback bookstores—every big city has them—and for ten or fifteen cents apiece get good books? Or better yet give the students money and let them go out and buy the books. Of one school Kozol says, "about a third of the school hours were spent at wandering in the schoolyard ('sports')...." But even in the most barren schoolyard there are plenty of things to do besides wander, and if we can for a few minutes stop wish-dreaming about gyms and swimming pools, we might be able to think of a few of them. In short, once we give up our excuses, and start seeing what we can do with what we have, we might surprise ourselves.

The second thing that blacks can do, and are beginning to do, for the education of their children, is to start their own schools. The New School for Children in Roxbury, even though its parent body is somewhat richer than most city blacks, is a good start in the right direction. Also promising are the Roxbury Community School of Boston, which serves a lower income parent body; the Children's Community, which for several years now, and with very little money, has been working in Ann Arbor, Michigan (though without more money, soon, it cannot survive): the Martin Luther King In-Community School in Berkeley, California, and others.

Finally, as we are beginning to see in I.S. 201 in Harlem, and in a few other parts of New York, blacks are beginning to try to find ways, even if they cannot control an entire public school system, to exercise effective control over the schools in their own neighborhoods, to get principals and teachers who will understand, respect, and meet the needs of their children, and to give the children the kind of pride and confidence in themselves, and the zest for learning and growth, that can be felt *only* by those who feel themselves part of an effective community. Such efforts are just beginning and they face great difficulties. They do not seem to me wasteful diversions of energy, but the very opposite. They are intensely practical, because they meet the problems of education directly, and where they are most difficult and serious.

The poorest children in Leicestershire are now among the best-educated children in Great Britain. Those who struggle to change the system here must set themselves no less a goal—that the poorest children of our predominantly black cities will be among the best-educated children in America.

—1967

COMIC TRUTH ON AN URGENT PROBLEM

The Way It Spozed to Be, by James Herndon.

James Herndon is a teacher. Some years ago he taught for one year in a ghetto junior high school. This is the story of that year. Of the many books I have read about teaching children, above all, poor city children, it is the best. It deals incisively with what is still the root problem of ghetto schools: their appalling failure to reach the kids, and the obsession with rote learning and imposed discipline which only drives them further into apathy and rebellion.

It is certainly the funniest book on the subject. Herndon is a gifted comic writer with a sharp eye and ear and the talent to make us see and hear what he has seen and heard. His descriptions are hilarious, as when he describes the "Plop Reflex," his girl pupils' secret weapon: whenever thwarted, they would launch themselves backward into space and crash on the floor. Yet Herndon does not use his school, or his pupils, or even his well-meaning and hopelessly incompetent principal as a mine for laughs. Like all true comic writers, he is deeply serious, and most funny when most serious. *The Way It Spozed to Be* is much funnier than *Up the Down Staircase* because it is more serious, honest, profound, concerned.

Of books about teaching it may well be the most helpful to teachers and would-be teachers. We are not much helped by hearing how brilliant people did miracles in the classroom. We are intimidated and burrow deeper into our nest of excuses—we're just ordinary folks, and anyway our kids are worse. But Herndon did no miracles; all he did was to get his students, after years of apathy and rebellion, to begin educating themselves. He had never taught before and had no special training or talents; we all have it in us to do what he did—if we want to. His kids—poor, black city kids—were as tough as anyone's. Unlike Herbert Kohl (*36 Children*), he did not even have his pupils all day and so could not build them a private, better world within the school. Each new day he had to break down, or get the children to take down, the barriers of indifference, resentment, defiance and despair that they had put between themselves and the world. There was no way to help his four nonreaders in class 7H to learn to read, because they would not admit they couldn't and would not take part in any activity that even seemed to hint that they couldn't, since "it was more honorable to appear bad than stupid."

Who, writing about the poor, talks about honor? Yet honor—the need to look good and, if you must look bad, to make sure someone else looks worse—moves these children. Having nothing to defend or hope for but appearances, they defend appearances at all costs. This book exposes the conflict between image and reality, between the way things "spozed to be" and the way they are. Back with his 7H class after a month's absence, Herndon heard the kids tell him how much better his substitute was than he.

Mrs. A. gave them work on the board every day, they screamed, and she made them keep a notebook with all this work in it and they were spozed to bring it every day to work in and get graded on it. That was what real teachers did, they told me. I asked to see some of the notebooks: naturally, no one had one. What about that? I asked. No use. She made us keep them notebooks, they all shouted. The fact that no one had kept or was keeping them notebooks didn't enter into it.

In the same way the principal complained, "...the children were not in their seats on time, they did not begin lessons promptly, many of them sat around doing nothing, there was not an atmosphere conducive to study...." Again, Herndon spoke for reality:

> I had to talk about results.... What was the good of
> saving all those materials...if at the end of the year
> they were all thrown out the window anyway? What
> good was the order of these experienced teachers if it

ended up in chaos? No one in my class had rioted, I
pointed out.... So who had the better control?

Again, no use. In school certain things are spozed to happen; the
kids are spozed to sit still, be quiet, read the texts, do the workbooks,
pass the exams. If none of these things happens, if the kids learn
nothing, riot in the halls, drop out, that's OK, as long as you tried to
make happen what spozed to happen. But if you tried to make something else happen, even if like Herndon's, your kind of order worked
and your kids found things worth doing and actually did them, you're
a threat to the system, and out you go. Out went Herndon. But the
story is not over. He has gone on teaching, and I hope he goes on
writing. We need him.

—1968

TALK

I REALLY CAN'T TELL YOU HOW pleased I am to be here, and by "here" I mean in Britain first of all, secondly in the County, and third on this Course. I would have to say that the things that have happened here, or at least those things I have seen happening here, seem to me to speak much more eloquently about education than I will be able to. That doesn't mean I'm not going to try to, but I do think that you have all probably learned first hand a great many of the things that I'm going to try to put into words.

The first thing that pops into my mind is that there has been a good deal of rather tiresome talk, certainly in my country and I suppose in yours, about what's called "Mini-Britain." There seems to be a lot of weeping and moaning in some quarters about Britain's decline from power. It seems to me, looking at this matter through the eyes of someone who has been very fond of this country since 1952, when I first came here as an adult, that this talk is misplaced. If we're going to look at the decline of Great Britain as an imperial world power, that decline was essentially accomplished and consummated in the years 1914 to 1918. Anything that's happened since seems to me to be but consequences stemming from it. Coming from a country that is trying to be an imperial power and having a pretty hard time of it, I'm not able to feel that the loss of your position as a world imperial power is, in fact, a great tragedy. I submit to you what many of you probably know much better than I do, that Britain may have an altogether different function and mission in today's world and one very much deserving of your support. That mission I see as twofold. In the first place I think it is possible for Britain to show that a large and highly industrialized country can he both free and civilized, and in the second place I think that Britain may have as a possible mission and function the job of providing the very much needed bridge between what is often called the white Western world and the much larger and much poorer but rapidly growing world of the black peoples. I don't know of any gulf which seems to me more serious than the rapidly deepening gulf between these two worlds. It has deepened economically in the last ten or fifteen years in spite of what has been done in the way of giving aid, and it seems to be deepening both inside of my country and outside of it both mentally and spiritually.

Well, this may seem to be a long way from education, but it isn't, because all of us in education are concerned with developing certain qualities of mind, of heart, and of spirit, and they have a great deal to do with Britain's position in the world today and its future, its possible mission. A case could be made, I think, that a certain kind of education, a certain kind of schooling, was appropriate for a nation which was deeply in the business of telling other people what to do, the business of being a colonial and imperial power. It may well have been that the public school tradition—I think of *Stalky and Co.*, a book which I've always enjoyed very much and oddly enough still do, although I don't sympathize with the Britain that Kipling was celebrating—it is possible that the Stalky and Co. education had a great deal to do with the things that most Englishmen wanted to do and had to do in those days. But what are called for now, I think, are rather different qualities. So I want to talk a little bit on this question of relevance. Probably most of us, as we consider our work, the things that we're trying to do, may feel that there exists somewhere a kind of conflict between the interests of society or the state and the interests of the child, and that for various reasons we have chosen to be on the side of the child. But we are worried because this conflict does exist and because we feel that so many of our colleagues are on the opposite side, and because we know that if the claims of the state or of society become sufficiently clamorous they will certainly override anything that seems as trivial to most people as do the needs and rights of children. So I want to suggest to you that this apparent conflict may not really exist at all.

Traditional methods of education, I think, have been based on a feeling that there is a body of knowledge and skill which we need to transmit to each new child, perhaps for the good of society, perhaps for the good of the child himself. Even in the so-called, and madly misnamed, revolution in education that's going on in my country, this has not really been very much challenged. In other words, by and large educators still agree that we adults ought to be deciding what every child is to be made to learn, and when he is to be made to learn it and how he is to be made to learn it, and we feel that it's our right and our job to decide how well he's learning it. Those of us who challenge this view are, at least at home, in a very small minority. I think there are more of you here, but not as many as you would like or I would like. Again, it seems to me that the historical case for this "body of knowledge" approach really doesn't exist any longer. It's been demolished by events. In this connection I think of a number of stories. One I heard very recently, in California. The man who told it had attended a meeting at which some of the leading people in California vocational education were talking to a large group of prominent businessmen, industrialists, employers of labor. At one point the chief of vocational education in the state of California said to these businessmen, "What we need to know from you gentlemen is what your employees are going to have to know seven years from now." He was greeted by what my informant describes as a burst of hysterical laughter. When it died down, a man from Lockheed Aircraft Corporation said, "I'm sorry, we can't tell you what our employees are going to need to know seven *months* from now." Now, it may very well be that the aircraft industry is changing technologically somewhat more rapidly than others, though not more rapidly than all others and certainly less rapidly than some. I think that what he said and what those other men implied by their laughter must be taken as a kind of fact of contemporary life.

I think of another thing that happened to me fairly recently. I was at a small dinner, with some half a dozen people, in Cambridge, Massachusetts. Two of the people there were physicists. One of them had got his degree at MIT and was working there at that time, and the other one happened to ask him what his field of study had been. The MIT man said, "Well, as a matter of fact I got my Ph.D. degree ten years ago in solid state physics, but I drifted out of the field and

I've been working in other kinds of things, and today I don't know what the solid state people are talking about." I find this quite a remarkable story. It seems to me that to go from a Ph.D. to almost total ignorance in a space of ten years is quite rapid progress! I think the story is important, because the fact is that whatever work he is doing in physics he was not trained to do during his academic training, or at least not directly. Subsequently I met in Illinois a young man who told me he had taken all his academic professional training in chemical engineering, but that he had very recently gone into electronics engineering, within the past six months, and was finding it very interesting. One might ask, as I did, how is it possible for him to do this? Why didn't he have to go to school and spend four years learning all the things that anyone would tell us electronics engineers have to know? He has found ways to bypass this problem. Presumably when he finds something that he needs to know he finds somebody who knows it and asks him. This seems to work very well. [Even more recently, I heard a man in a Boston restaurant tell another that "the money" was in educating engineers, because "five years after an engineer gets his degree he's out of date."]

Quite recently a hook that many of you know, particularly the scientific people, *The Double Helix*, has received a lot of attention at home. I've ordered it. I haven't got a copy yet, so I haven't read it. I mean to. I even probably will. So far I've only read reviews of it, but they have interested me because a number of them have pointed out that Watson and Crick were totally ignorant of a great many important fields of knowledge which one would have supposed they needed to know, which in fact they did need to know, in order to discover what they did about the DNA molecule that they made. By our usual standards of looking at these things they were hopelessly unqualified to discover this. That is to say, by the traditional ways of deciding what qualifications are. Now of course they were supremely well qualified, because they brought to their task qualities which are not picked up in school and in fact rarely survive school: a deep and wide-ranging curiosity; a profound, not to say arrogant confidence in their own ability to learn things and to figure things out; a very considerable resourcefulness at finding out how to find out things. And armed with these valuable resources, and a not inconsiderable amount of knowledge, they were able to discover what they discovered.

I can think of many examples like this. What they add up to is this: the body of knowledge is growing so rapidly that in the first place it's absolutely inconceivable that any human being now or at any time in the future will be able to encompass more than some tiny fraction of it. This is a fairly recent development. Even as recently as the 1920s when Huxley was writing most of his best novels, I think it was possible for a man as brilliant as he was, and with leisure and many scientific connections and a real thirst for learning, to feel that he was at least reasonably close to the frontier of learning in most of the major fields of human study. I'm sure that he *felt* that he knew most of what any people knew and I think he may have been fairly right. But in the last forty years this possibility has long since gone. What we think of as our fields of learning or our disciplines, as the academics like to call them, are rapidly subdividing into little sections which find it increasingly difficult to talk to each other. I was told not long ago by an anthropologist, a man doing graduate work in it, that anthropology was beginning to divide up into four or five quite separate and distinct fields, each with its own approach to the discipline, each fiercely intolerant of the others. And so forth and so forth. I think we can expect to see this continue. So the idea of the Renaissance man who encompasses some important part of the body of knowledge in his mind is gone. This is not possible. We can only know a tiny part of the sum of human knowledge. We are all of us, no matter how hard we work, no matter how curious we are, condemned to grow relatively more ignorant every day we live, to know less and less of the sum of what is known.

Now, the next thing is that a great deal of what we know at any time is very soon going to be out of date. In other words, knowledge is not only growing with enormous rapidity, it is obsolescing with enormous rapidity. This has been true even in our lifetime. I studied physics at school; in my last year I took a preliminary college course, and we used one of the most up-to date college physics texts of the time. On page one it told us that the fundamental law of physics is that matter is not created or destroyed. This was about 1938. We had to scratch the statement out even before the end of the year, because in fact matter was destroyed in a laboratory about that time. I was compelled by the powers that be to study chemistry, because everybody knew that chemistry is good for you. The other day I happened to mention to a friend of mine, who studied his chemistry much more recently and who is now a teacher of chemistry, that the only thing I could really remember out of my chemistry was valence. He laughed the kind of laugh which in this country is, or used to be, called a snigger, and said, "You're older than you look. Chemists haven't talked about valence for *years*." Well, that particular piece of learning was not one I was terribly sorry to let go. But it makes you think. Even a great deal of what I was taught about classical history, Greek and Roman history, historians no longer believe to be true. If you can believe it, I still grew up in the day when historians used to talk about the Greeks building chaste, white temples. Of course, thanks to people like Kitto and others we now know that they were covered with gold and red and blue paint and if they'd had neon signs they'd have put them up too.

So there's not only vastly more to be known than any of us can know, but an enormous amount of what we know at any particular time is fairly soon going to be found to be either partially untrue or wholly untrue or useless. And the question is, how in fact do we survive in this situation? One is tempted to say, as many people do say, that the only thing to do in this circumstance is to throw up our hands and simply let the experts decide everything. But a casual look at the front page of the daily paper reveals why that isn't such a good idea either. The experts are, in the first place, in profound disagreement about what needs to be done, and in the second place, even where they agree they don't seem to come out very well. Indeed, there is a very important reason why the holders of expert knowledge may he peculiarly unfitted for dealing with the kind of world we live in. It is precisely because they have spent so long and worked so hard learning the things that they think they know that they are unwilling to look at or consider or think about a world in which those things may not be true any more. It's the expert who is liable to cling to a past which no longer exists, to a condition which has changed.

We see this problem in our own country in the field of education in many ways. Two instances come to my mind with particular force.

About two years ago our Federal government published a report generally known as the Coleman report, about inequality of educational opportunity. This was based on massive stacks of research done over a great many years. It took the report a long time to come out. It's a most impressive document, and most of our educational experts are basing all of their thinking about urban education and its problems on the report. But the trouble is that the report is already, in vital respects, out of date. The situation has changed so radically, the relationships between our own black and white communities, the aspirations of the black community, and the leadership of both communities have changed so rapidly, that anybody who relies heavily on the report for ideas is going to be out of the picture. And this is going to be particularly true in social affairs. By the time the experts have collected enough data to feel that they're sure of what they're doing, the situation will have changed and they will no longer be doing the right thing.

Well, the question then is, if piling up bodies of knowledge and expert data—if packing our heads full of ideas faster and faster—is not the answer, what is it, then, we have to do? In this connection I think of a letter a student of mine wrote me when she was in college. I had taught this girl in what we call the ninth grade, that would be your third form, and again in eleventh grade, your fifth form. When she was in her second year of college she wrote me a letter, talking of many things, and at one point she said, "What I envy about you, John, is that you have everything all taped." This is American slang by which she meant that I had everything all figured out, in its place, organized, and so forth. Now, I don't blame her for feeling this. This is precisely the picture that most educators try to give children of what it means to be educated: that you have everything all taped. You not only know everything, you know where it fits and how its parts relate to each other. This poor girl, in her confusion and ignorance and bafflement, wrote how much she envied me. I supposedly had everything all figured out. I wrote her back and said, "You could not possibly be more mistaken. The difference between you and me is not that I have everything all taped, it's that I know I don't and I never will, I don't expect to and I don't need to. I expect to live my entire life about as ignorant and uncertain and confused as I am now, and I have learned to live with this, not to worry about it. I have learned to swim in uncertainty the way a fish swims in water." It seems to me that it is only in this way that it is possible to live in the kind of rapidly changing world that we live in. We are obliged to act, in the first place, and in the second place to act intelligently, or as intelligently as possible, in a world in which, as I say, we know very little, in which, even if the experts know more than we do, we have no way of knowing which expert knows the most. In other words, we are obliged to live out our lives thinking, acting, judging on the basis of the most fragmentary and uncertain and temporary information.

The point of all this is that this is what very young children are good at doing. This is why the things that I've been saying about the learning of young children seem to me now to be relevant to what we're thinking about the learning of anybody and everybody. The very young child faces a world which is, by and large, totally incomprehensible, just a "blooming, buzzing confusion." But he's not afraid of this confusion. He doesn't feel that he has to have it all taped. He is not only able but eager to reach out into this world that doesn't make any sense to him, and to take it in. And furthermore, he doesn't even feel a neurotic compulsion to get it taped, to get it all patterned, structured, conceptualized, so that he can say, this is this, and this fits this, and this happens because of this. He is willing to tolerate misunderstanding, to suspend judgement, to wait for patterns to emerge, for enlightenment to come to him. I think children learn by a process of continuous revelation much more than by analysis. And, indeed, for facing situations of enormous complexity traditional methods of analytic thinking are really of no use to us. Where you have a hundred variables, none of which are under your exact control, how do you, by systematic, analytic processes, get the thing organized? It can't be done, and the enormous strength of children's thinking lies in the fact that they don't try to do it. They face, and not just face but move out joyously, eagerly, into this extraordinary confusion and doubt and uncertainty. They take it in and they wait for the patterns and similarities and regularities of that world to appear. The young child does all the time the kind of thing which is so hard for us to do and which we must learn to do. The young child is continually building what I like to call a mental model of the world, the universe, and then checking it against reality as it presents itself to him, and then tearing it down and rebuilding it as necessary, and then checking again and tearing it down and rebuilding it and checking again. He goes through this process I have no idea how many times a year or even a day, and he's not afraid to do it. What happens to him later, to a very considerable extent as a result of his schooling, is that he begins to get such a vested interest in this mental model, whatever it may be, that he becomes increasingly unwilling to consider or look at or hear about whatever doesn't fit into it. It becomes a bed of Procrustes. Everything has got to be stretched or chopped to fit. So there's a very real sense in which we have got to learn to do—I say "we" meaning everybody who is not a young child, both ourselves and our older students—we have got to learn to do what the young child is already good at doing, what every child is born good at doing, this business of continually comparing our mental model, our structure of reality, against reality and being willing to check it, modify it, change it, in order to take account of circumstances. It seems to me that it is only people with these qualities of mind who can abandon the panicky quest for certainty and understanding and order and who will be willing to swim, to suspend themselves—I think of a bird in air or a fish in water—in the uncertainty and confusion and ignorance and bafflement in which it is our fate to live for the rest of our lives. It is only these people who are going to be able to think sensibly about whatever it is we have to think about.

Now, I'm going to stop talking, but for those of you who may be interested I'd be delighted to continue the conversation for as long as anybody wants. You see, what I'm leading up to is this: I don't believe in the curriculum, I don't believe in grades, I don't believe in teacher-judged learning. I believe in children learning with our assistance and encouragement the things they want to learn, when they want to learn them, how they want to learn them, why they want to learn them. This is what it seems to me education must now be about.

Question: You mentioned the model of reality that is tested against the real world, and you mentioned an analytical method which you seemed to think was a bad way of going about things—

Answer: Oh, it's all right for certain kinds of situations. By analytical I mean in the laboratory sense: if this particular event may be caused by any one of five causes we isolate them one by one, we isolate the variables and see which things remain constant. This is a very useful procedure in situations where the variables are reasonably limited and where they are under our control, where they're not inextricably interconnected. When we try to apply this method in a field like psychology, and try to act as if we were chemists or physicists looking at the human mind, we just make ourselves ridiculous, I think. Obviously, most psychologists don't think that. But I think they will. You see, I don't believe in psychological measurement. Of any kind. I don't think it can be done.

Question: Do you believe in compulsory schooling?

Answer: Oddly enough, I don't. It's only in the last two months, really, that I've begun to think about that question. Until then I had accepted compulsory school attendance as a kind of given, which it was simply not within our power to change. What made me begin to ask myself whether it really was an unchangeable given was an increasingly long series of conversations with agonized parents in the States, all of them saying, or writing, in one way or another, "My child is being destroyed in school, and what can I do about it?" The possible answers are long. The law talks about "exhausting all possible remedies," and there are quite a number to be exhausted. I found myself saying, "If none of these work, if there is really no alternative, I would suggest you start seeing how much you can keep your child out of school. You may be able to challenge the demand on the school's part that he be there." It seemed to me, at least within our own framework of law, that this might very well be a civil liberties question. The justification for the schools and for compulsory attendance is that the schools are doing things which help children. In a case where this is manifestly not so, they have very little grounds for demanding that a child be there. I began to think about the thing further and I began to feel that these laws do not really work in the best interests of the schools or the teachers either. In our country, and I guess it's the same here, the effect of the compulsory school attendance laws is to turn the schools into jails. This is very difficult. To the extent that kids are there only because they are compelled to be, enormous and expensive problems arise. We have big problems of vandalism in our cities, and in fact it's a commonplace in most parts of

America to see schools surrounded by what we call a cyclone fence, a burglarproof fence. I like to say that in the States if you see a cyclone fence around a piece of property you know that you're looking either at one of the installations of the United States Government or at a public school. This is sad. I heard the superintendent of schools in one of our big cities talk about the number of millions of dollars he had to spend repairing broken windows every year. Well, who breaks them? Kids break them. Why do they break them? They break them because they hate those damned buildings. Years ago there was a poem written in the United States called "Factory Windows Are Always Broken." I can only remember the last two lines of it: "Something, it seems, is rotten in Denmark. / End of the factory window song." The gist of the poem was that factory windows were broken because people hated factories and the people who ran factories had better get busy and start thinking about it. I think the same thing is very much true of schools. And even aside from the vandalism, we have, and you probably have, all kinds of special correctional schools: this jailing business gets very complicated and expensive. All kinds of records have got to be kept to show that the prisoners are all in the jail when they are supposed to be, or if not, where they are and whether or not they have a right to be where they are. And of course, from the point of view of the teacher, I'm afraid you all know what it does to the classroom to have even one or two people in it who *desperately* don't want to be there. It's spoiled for you, for them, for the other children. They make trouble far out of proportion to their numbers.

Now, I'm not in the crystal ball business. I'm perfectly willing to speculate about what kinds of things might happen if compulsory school attendance laws were, in fact, relaxed or done away with, what other institutions might arise to occupy these children, what changes might be made in the schools themselves in order to get kids in. Incidentally, in our country, at least, we have the ironical situation, in many of our cities, that having spent ten years making the children hate school so much that they drop out, we then spend all kinds of money trying to figure out how to make schools attractive enough so that they'll come back in. Maybe something should have been done sooner. Maybe if children could stay away from school when they felt they weren't getting anything out of it, we educators would get the message a little sooner that something needed to be done in that factory. I would also say on the basis of my own experience as a teacher that I think it's a kind of arrogant nonsense for us educators to assume that any day a child doesn't spend in school is a day lost and wasted. There are lots of places where children learn outside of school. I can remember that when my friend Bill's youngest daughter was first starting to go to school there were days when she would say she didn't want to go because she was too busy. And she was! She had more important things to do. I think that's fine. So, at any rate, there I am. I don't know how that's going to work out. It may be a long time before anything is changed. It may not be changeable. But at least in my own country I'm beginning to talk and write about it.

Question: You have no practical program how one might reach this state of affairs?

Answer: I don't know what the law is in this country. In my own country, these laws are passed by state legislators. I think that they could be overturned there though I rather doubt that's where it's going to begin. I think in my own country they might possibly be challenged in the courts. Nobody has ever made such a challenge. The history of the development of our own law tends to show that when such challenges are made they very often lose the first time around. By and large rights are created, in a democratic society, when enough people insist on them, when they begin to be willing to go to enough trouble to get them. Aside from that, even with the law existing as it stands it may be possible to arrive at some kind of accommodations with local schools.

Question: If you made holidays a little longer, and then opened schools on a voluntary basis, not for the whole holiday, perhaps for three weeks, you might then demonstrate that when schools are open children will come in. In other words, you would give an example in advance of demanding legislation.

Answer: Yes, I think that's a good point. Now, there are places in our country, of course, as there are here, where rather different schools are run during holidays. But, as so often happens, it's the rich who get the enrichment. It's in the places where the schools are ordinarily the least bad that there are likely to be very interesting summer sessions.

They don't take place, often, where they are most needed. Still, I think they are important. There is also beginning to grow in the States a radical movement in private education. When I say it's radical, I mean radical in two senses. It's radical in the Summerhillian or libertarian sense of being based on the principle that kids ought to learn what and when and how they want to. It's radical in another sense, in that the people who are starting these schools, many of them very young, are beginning to think in terms of their school being in or near a city, of being day schools rather than boarding schools, of being open to the whole community, of being schools with porous walls so that the students can go out into the community and the community can come into the school. Perhaps most of all, they are trying to do their work on a budget per pupil comparable to that spent by the state supported schools, so that whatever lessons they seem to be learning can be applied in public education if public education wants to apply them. There aren't many of these schools, but there are quite a few of them and there are more of them starting all the time. I get letters about this from people all over the country. And it may very well be that in such schools we will have the real kind of educational laboratory and demonstration centers which in your country, I guess, are supplied by many of the state schools. We don't have anything comparable to Leicestershire in the States.

Question: Don't you think that while many of us might agree with this idea of obsolete bodies of knowledge, competition for jobs is getting harder and harder, employers are demanding tokens that children have learned X amount? If we're going to adopt these ideas, aren't we letting the children down in this sense?

Answer: You might be if you did nothing else, but of course it seems to me that public education means educating the public, and not just the public's children. I think that some employers are beginning to feel what the man from Lockheed felt. It may very well be that this employer from Lockheed, whose employees have to learn something completely different every six months, has not yet figured out what this means in terms of school education, in which case it seems to me it's somebody's job to point it out to him. I think it is at least possible that we may be able to convince employers, and particularly in industries which do change very rapidly, that it is not going to be possible to prepare children in school for a lifetime of work, and that the attempt will do very much more harm than good. And also, simply because of the expensiveness of a great deal of modern equipment and the rate at which it becomes obsolete, it's not going to be possible to put in our school buildings, or our vocational training schools, the kind of tools and equipment that people are going to be working with.

In other words, I think we are going to find ourselves in a great many fields going back to something much closer to an apprentice form of training. Interestingly enough, people are beginning to realize this in the States in the training of doctors. There is a great dissatisfaction among many doctors with the traditional four years of medical school, two years of internship, and so on. They are beginning to realize that the body of medical knowledge has grown to be vastly greater than anything a student can encompass in four years of medical school. The most recent development that I have heard of in medical school education runs about like this: in this school each incoming student will be assigned, under the supervision of a qualified senior doctor, to an entire family. He will be not finally but immediately responsible for the health of that entire family and that family will be, so to speak, the core of his medical curriculum. Now, he'll still have lots of books, but the things he studies and the questions he asks and the laboratories he goes to and the things that he finds out he's going to look for and ask and find out because they have something to do with the health of these real, live people. This, it seems to me, is a kind of apprenticeship. And I rather suspect that something like this will continue.

Again, in technical education, our education in scientific fields assumes that you cannot do advanced work out on the frontier of science unless you've begun at square one, so to speak, and gone every step of the way all along. But the journey is getting too long. In plain fact, there are people like my friend in solid-state physics who begin to work in a different field very close to the frontier, or the young man in chemical engineering, or Crick and Watson, the Nobel Prize winners. As the distance from square one to the frontier gets longer and longer we're going to have to find more and more ways to cut in as close as possible to the place where we're doing the work. I would add, too, that even in terms of the most conventional exam-taking I don't think there has been any particular evidence to show that children learning out of their own curiosity are very much worse off, if any worse off at all, than conventionally educated children. But that dodges the issue a little bit. I do think we have to educate the public about the inappropriateness of traditional education.

Question: How would you keep an army and an air force? I preface this by saying that I disagree entirely with what you've been saying. How would a country that adopted what you are saying keep them?

Answer: Well, I'm not sure how they do now. I don't know whether your implication is that under this system of education nobody would want to go in the army or if they did go they wouldn't be able to—

Question: It's both that but also this: our present system of education is dedicated to the body-of-knowledge concept.

Answer: Yes, there is an extent to which traditional education is, to put it as boldly as possible, a preparation for slavery. You know: "Orders is orders," and you're going to spend all your life taking orders so you might as will start from age six. And, indeed, I often get this argument. When I meet somebody, as I do quite often, who believes that all this talk about freedom in your country and mine doesn't really amount to anything, that in fact life *is* slavery and the sooner kids get used to it the better, when I meet people who talk this way, I try to say something like this: If I were in your shoes and really believed that somehow I had lost any important freedom of choice in my own life, that I was, in fact, a kind of well-paid slave, I would want to educate my child for something better. Where this "sentimental" appeal fails, well, there are gulfs, which cannot be bridged or filled with words: there are plenty of souls that aren't going to be saved. But I think it is possible to say to the Establishment that it is not really well served by these kinds of order-takers, because things are too complicated. A man I know in the States likes to terrify large groups of schoolteachers by saying "Any teacher who can be replaced by a machine should be." And to this I add that any teacher who can be replaced by a machine *will* be. And not only any teacher, but *anyone.* Jobs that can be done on the basis of memorized information, memorized procedures—you do this, you do that—it is really very easy and it's going to become increasingly easy to work out some way to get a little machine to do them. The one thing that human beings can do that machines will never be able to do is to think originally about new and changing situations, and I would say that the kinds of skills and order-taking abilities which at one time were useful to the Establishment are just going to be increasingly un-useful.

Question: Where do you see structure and certainty arising in the society you describe? You have compared the way in which we ought to approach our environment to the way a young child naturally responds to a highly complex system that it encounters. But this young child does possess considerable certainty and security in his parents. Do you see any comparable structures in our society to which we can cling? Or any to which you suggest we should?

Answer: If there are patterns, regularities, structures in society, children will discover them. Now, I realize this is only indirectly an answer to your question, but your question is close enough to a question I get asked so frequently that I'll answer them both at the same time. Sometimes I get asked, often by people trained in science, "Aren't you asking every child to invent the wheel all over again?" The last time I was asked that question I was in a high school in Connecticut, and the man with whom I was talking and I were standing in the front hall of a school looking out through big glass doors into the school parking lot, where there were about fifty automobiles with four visible wheels each. I pointed out the door and said, "They don't have to invent the wheel, it's been invented, it's out there, they'll notice it." Whatever regularities, patterns, structures, and so forth do exist in our society can be and will be discovered by people living in it.

Question: Since you have described the uncertainty and flux of our society, would you care to attempt the more difficult definition of the structures, which presumably do exist?

Answer: One of the things that make life difficult in your country and even more so in mine, a thing which I think contributes enormously to the very great spiritual unease of Americans, and will, I think, increasingly to that of other countries as they go down the same paths, is the fact that a lot of the invariants, the unchangeables, the tried-and-true, the certainties on which men used to stand, the kinds of things people used to be able to hold onto to keep their balance in this rocking, shifting world—these things are disappearing. We are going to have to learn to get along with fewer certainties, because there aren't going to be as many. Now, I do get asked questions about the cultural traditions and the functions of education to pass along the cultural heritage, or a set of values; but the great fact of life in my own country, less so here but I suspect considerably and increasingly so, is that traditional morality, values, and culture as a real guide for human life have long since ceased to exist. In point of fact, we are *not* guided, sustained, supported by the things, which we claim to believe in. This is what makes life very difficult for young people, and I think one of the things we are going to have to do in some way is to re-create values, maybe the same values.

Question: Might it, therefore, be a little unfair to offer the young child as a model and an example to us, since the young child does in fact possess a fair amount of security in the kind of exploration he keeps carrying out?

Answer: He may. The amount of security young children possess varies considerably from one to another. You're perfectly right, but on the other hand the young child is in fact physically much more helpless and dependent than we are. We have a kind of responsibility—how shall I put it—to be braver than little children, even if the world is rocking around underneath us and there's nothing much to hold on to. You just cling to the deck the best way you can.

Question: Apart from the different role in which you see Britain, does this deal with the situation? Hasn't it just accelerated? So the problems which faced educators who thought about education previously are still the same.

Answer: But they are much more urgent and increasing ever more rapidly. The case for traditional education seems to me much weaker than it has been, and is getting ever weaker, and the case for an education which will give a child primarily not knowledge and certainty but resourcefulness, flexibility, curiosity, skill in learning, readiness to unlearn—the case for very much the sort of thing that's happening here—grows ever stronger. This is not something which well-meaning people have cooked up because they feel kindly in their hearts toward children, although I think that's a very important reason. But we have other ways of defending what we're doing. And I think this is important.

Question: Could I ask something which might put you on the spot a bit? You say that there is no longer the body of knowledge which needs to be learned. If we confined this to the primary school for the moment, do you think there are areas of experience through which all children should go?

Answer: This is a very difficult question, and it's difficult because I myself am in a state of great doubt and confusion. Things that I thought I was sure about three years ago I've become unsure about, and things I thought I was reasonably sure about even a year ago I am relatively uncertain about. I am much less convinced than I once was, for example, of the usefulness of mathematics, either as a preparation for life or even as a tool to help the intellectual growth of the child. I think that in my first book I said something to the effect that mathematics may be a way by which children's intelligence may be developed. I still think that for some children it may be, but I am rather inclined to doubt that this is the best way for most children. I think there are many other modes of learning. I suspect that the kind of simultaneous work in different media we did this afternoon in the music-art-poetry class may be far more important in terms of human growth and development, far more important in terms of the growth of human capacity, than the kinds of clever tricks I once used to be able to do, or get children to do, with Cuisenaire rods or this, that, and the other. I still rather like mathematics. Maybe I could put it this way. When I was talking to the Association of Teachers of Mathematics in London I said that it seems to me that we have to think very carefully about the question of whether mathematics is some kind of necessity or whether it's an entertainment. I think a very good case can be made for it as an entertainment, rather like music. I happen to love music. But I think that a person who loves chess, or doing mathematics puzzles or problems or proofs, is getting the kind of aesthetic satisfaction that I get listening to great music, and as far as I'm concerned it's as good as mine, and every bit as much worth encouraging. But when we talk about mathematics, whether arithmetic or in some loftier form, as a necessity for intelligent human life in the twentieth century, I part company. I think arithmetic in my country is largely a useless skill. Almost all of the figuring done in the United States is done by machines and will be done so increasingly. This is probably less true here but will become more so. I suspect that within twenty years we will have things the size of a transistor radio—you're afflicted with them here, I guess—which will do all the operations, and more, that are now contained in the school mathematics curriculum. Not just the basic operations but square roots and who knows what. And they won't be terribly expensive. It will seem ridiculous to teach people to do arithmetic, and on a loftier plane algebra, geometry, trigonometry, solid geometry, calculus. As I consider what seem to me to be the major problems of contemporary society in my country and your country, I can really think of none of which I would say that greater or lesser mathematical knowledge would enable people to think better or worse about them. I even doubt that there is a particularly strong connection between the kinds of mathematics taught in schools and the kinds of mathematical work that are really being done at the front levels of engineering and technology and so forth. I don't think what you learn in school would help you to program a computer, and if our feeling is that in order to prepare children for working in a computer age they've got to learn computer skills, the way to do it is to get them working on computers. I don't see how factoring quadratic equations enters into the picture.

Question: Would you treat the skill of reading in the same way?

Answer: No, reading is something different. But here's another of the bombshells which I'm hurling freely all over the United States, so I might as well hurl it here, though I think it will cause somewhat less trauma here than it usually does in the United States. I quite firmly believe that, with the possible exception of children in a very remote rural environment, most children would learn to read if nothing were done about it at all. With children living in an environment full of print, newspapers, magazines, writing on television, signs, advertising, I cannot imagine how any child who had not been made to feel he was too stupid to learn to read would not learn. Now, in fact I think there are things that can be done in a school environment, and many of your schools do them, which will make it easier for a child to make the kinds of explorations and discoveries in reading that he earlier made in speaking. But I not only don't think that reading needs to be taught, I think most of what we consider to be our reading problems, our reading difficulties, arise out of the teaching rather than out of the inherent difficulty of the work. Viewed as an intellectual task, the task of learning to read—of breaking the phonic code, of putting together the some 45 sounds of spoken English and the some 380 signs of written English—doesn't compare with the task of learning to speak, which children sort out for themselves. So I don't think it needs to be taught.

Question: You could perhaps reverse the skills and have the same problem. If children learned to read in the ways they learned to speak and then you brought in speech later, you would have problems with speech. You can't perhaps consider a skill in isolation from the way it is learned. Children simply can't learn to read in the ways they learned to speak.

Answer: I may not understand you. They can't learn to read in the way they learn to speak—

Question: Unless they learn at the same time.

Answer: What I mean by "in the same way" is this. A number of things are involved in a child's learning to speak. He takes in a great deal of raw speech data from the world around him. He begins to sort these out in his own mind into grammatical patterns. By the way, I've heard linguists who've made a study of the early speech learning of children say that they think children learn the grammar before they learn the words. They get a feeling about the way the language is put together before they know what the individual units mean. I won't belabor that point, except to say that one of the things that children do is abstract out of all this speech they hear around them the grammatical points of the language. They make mental models of the grammar of English. At first these models are very crude, and they try them out and make mistakes and realize that they've got to be refined. By the time they're six years old or so they have about 90 or 95 percent of the grammar worked out. They also go through another highly original and inventive process. They start out facing a world of discrete objects, just a huge variety of things, and before children begin to name objects they have to begin to create classes in their mind. The word "concept" is very popular in America, and there's a lot of high-flown talk about "concept formation in school." But the fact is that when the child first says the word "chair" he has already created the concept "chair." He's not calling the chair "chair" the way you might call a brother "Bill." When he points to a chair and says "chair" he has already figured out for himself that the chair is one of a whole great class, as we would call it, of chairs, somewhat different from tables and benches and bureaus and pianos. This is classification of the world, breaking things down into taxonomies, finding the right label for each. He gets the sounds of the labels from us, but he has to decide which labels go with which. Children learn the names of very few things by being taught to them. All this learning comes about by a process of exploration and invention and trial-and-error and correction. And this is what I mean by doing it in the same way. The child can do this same kind of thing in the world of reading. "What does that say, and what does that say?" and from these he would abstract relationships between written letters and spoken sounds. He would begin to put the phonic patterns together.

Question: You said that in learning to speak children did it by correction, they weren't taught.

Answer: Ah, but they do the correction.

Question: I think you're wrong there. You say a chair is called "a chair" and one distinguishing feature is that it has four legs, but then, so has a horse, and you often get horses called "cats" by young children or other men called "daddy." And they are corrected. They don't correct themselves.

Answer: They *do* correct themselves. I've known many more young children than you have: forgive me for pulling that kind of rank on you, but I know lots of families, I am a frequent guest in a great many families who have young children, and one of the things that I've been observing for a long, long time is the phenomenon of young children learning to speak. One of the things I have seen is that most of these kinds of corrections they make for themselves. In fact, many speech therapists, at least in our country, seem to believe now that children who are very rigorously corrected by their parents will either stop talking or be inclined to develop stammers or stutters. They think this is the origin of a great many of these kinds of speech defects. Now, I don't say that this is true in one hundred percent of the cases. There are probably some families which do instantly correct every mistake in the speech of their children—I think it's an error to do it, it's unwise—but there may be children who survive this merciless and really very discourteous treatment without being damaged. But with the large number of small children I've observed in their native habitat, people don't correct their speech all the time; maybe because they're too lazy, maybe because they're courteous, I don't know why.

Question: Isn't it also a fact that the way adults talk to children when they're learning to speak is very important in the kind of language they develop?

Answer: Oh yes, the language that a child will learn is the language he hears around him. I don't mean to say that a child invents language out of whole cloth, though there are children who do. I met somebody not very long ago who told me about a six-year-old girl who speaks almost entirely a private language that her parents and a few people in the family can understand, but who speaks very little English. And there are on record, I think, a good many cases of identical twins who until about the age of seven spoke a private language which nobody else understood. However, generally speaking, the language which children do learn is the language that's spoken around them, and if it's a dialect or a substandard form of the language, that's the one they learn. You're perfectly right about that.

Question: Apart from fewer broken windows, do you think that a society made up of children who had grown up into adults, who had been educated in ways you suggest, would be different in many ways from contemporary society?

Answer: Yes, I do, and I have to say that I think it would be very much better. You see, it has come to me fairly recently, and with really shocking impact, that the things we do in the name of education—and I mean "we" in the larger sense—probably are to a devastating degree destructive of spirit, character, identity. The harm I think we do goes much deeper than the kinds of bad intellectual strategies that I talked about in *How Children Fail*. It is intellectual, but it's much more than that. There's a man in Great Britain of whom many of you may know, named R. D. Laing. He's a psychiatrist, and an expert, insofar as anybody is, in the field of schizophrenia. He has written a book called *The Politics of Experience*. I only recently read it and it bowled me over. He pointed out something that, being ignorant about mental treatment, I didn't know, or hadn't thought about. He said that the treatment of people we choose to label "schizophrenics" is almost wholly based, in his phrase, on "the invalidation of their experience." Now, what does he mean by this? He means that we, the self-labeled "healthy" people, say to the schizophrenics, labeled by us the "sick" people, "Your way of perceiving the world, your way of feeling about it, your way of communicating about it, your way of reacting to it, are wrong, sick, crazy. You've got to learn to see things the way we do and react to them the way we do, and then when you do that you're going to be healthy and fine and we'll let you out of here." And of course under those circumstances they don't get let out, because they don't get well under those circumstances. This assumption itself, this way of treating another human being, is itself more destructive than anything else could be. Well, I read that with what the French call a *frisson*, a shudder of horror, because I suddenly saw what I'd never thought of before, which is that our treatment of young children in most schools, and even before school—it goes on in the home, too—essentially invalidates their experience. What we do in the school (never mind what nice things we preach) says in effect to young children, "Your experience, your concern, your hopes, your fears, your desires, your interests, they count for nothing. What counts is what we are interested in, what we care about, and what we have decided you are to learn."

This, as I think about it, seems to be a kind of spiritual lobotomy. A person who can grow up through this with any very strong feeling of identity and esteem and self-respect and of personal dignity and worth is a truly remarkable person. In fact, the children I have taught, and I have taught only in rather stylish private schools in the States, at the uppermost level of education—the children I've taught, by all standards the most favored children of our country, did not have any strong sense of their identity and their worth and their dignity. They were indeed robbed of something tremendously important. I think we are beginning to see in our country a reaction to this (and by the way I am very sympathetic to the teenagers and student revolutionaries and even the poor hippies). What troubles me about the rebellion of the young against society is that by and large it seems to me a very destructive one: it's a self-immolating rebellion, for the most part. [I feel this much less now (Winter 1969). In fact, I think the rebellion of the young is one of the most hopeful and constructive phenomena of our times.] But again, it seems to me, thinking of the kids I've known, that they spend so much of their growing lives either *doing* what people tell them to do or *not* doing it, they spend so much of their time reacting in one way or another to those external pressures, that they have very little time to find out who and what they are.

You may ask, wasn't this always true of school? And I would say, perhaps it was, but school did not always eat up all of a child's life. As Paul Goodman pointed out, at the turn of the century in America only six per cent of each growing generation finished high school, let alone college. Even in the 1920s in our country, the percentage wasn't much more than that. So a child found out who he was and what he could do, and got some kind of feeling about his worth as a human being, out in the world. And those particular people who were good at the scholastic game, who liked books and who could do all these things, went on to certain specialized kinds of jobs. But in our country we have crammed everybody into this great cider-squeezing machine. And it's enormously destructive.

Here I go back to the kinds of things I was talking about. I think the problems of racial tension, the problems of poverty, if they're going to be solved at all, require people who are so much more at ease and at home with themselves than most of us are, who are so much freer of anger and envy and despair, that they're going to be able to act with the magnanimity and far-sightedness that are called for. The human race can't go on as it is. I don't know what time is allotted to us, but what we've got to have within a reasonably near future is almost a radical new kind of human being.

Question: How would you set about getting the quantities of teachers that are clearly required to operate in the system you describe?

Answer: Generally speaking, I think that teachers have got to be given, in their training, the kinds of experiences we want them later to give to their children. I think they have got to be allowed to discover the pleasure and excitement of learning things for their own reasons in their own way. This coming year I am going to be teaching some education courses, one at Harvard in the fall term and a couple at the University of California in the winter term. One of the things I'm going to try to do is to put into practice what I'm talking about. I'm not going to have required assignments, tests, and grades. I'm going to give people a list of resources, and by resources I not only mean books to read but schools to visit and people to talk to and places to investigate. I'm going to say: if you want to know more about any of these I'll tell you more, and if you want to talk about any of the things you've read or seen or investigated I'll be delighted to join you in these discussions; but *Explore!* There's what's being done, get out and look at it. This seems to me essentially the way it's going to have to be done. It's going to be difficult.

[Some students did not like it, some dropped out of it, but many found it an important and exciting experience.]

—1968

LETTER

—1968

Dear Dr. Bliss:

...I think children learn better when they learn what they want to learn when they want to learn it, and how they want to learn it, learning for their own curiosity and not at somebody else's order. I believe that learning would be greatly improved if we could completely or at least largely abolish the fixed curriculum in its present sense. I do not believe that testing and grading form any inherent or useful function in learning; in fact, they corrupt and impede the learning process. I am altogether opposed to any kind of so-called ability grouping in school. I think that in many more cases than not it is the act of instruction itself that impedes learning and nowhere else more than in the field of reading; in short, I feel that children would learn to read better and more easily if they were not taught. I think we need to find ways to get more people into the schools who are not teachers. I do not think it is helpful to have children spend all their time with people who have no other concerns than children. I would like to see streams of people coming into the schools who are there to talk about their outside life and work in the world. I would also like to see children encouraged and helped to use the resources of the world outside the school to further their learning. I believe that compulsory school attendance no longer serves a useful function, either to schools, teachers or students, and that it should be done away with or greatly modified. I think we have made education, which should be something that helps young people move into the world and do useful work there, into an enormous obstacle standing in their way, and I think we need to find ways to remove that obstacle. In short, I am opposed to all kinds of credential requirements as preconditions for doing work. I think we should remove every possible obstacle between any child and any gainful or useful contribution he wants to make to society. Everything we say and do tends to separate learning from living, and we should try instead to join them together...

Sincerely yours,

John Holt

BIBLIOGRAPHY

Education

Dennison, George, *The Lives of Children*. New York, Random House, Spring, 1969.

Epstein, Jason, articles on the New York City Schools. *The New York Review of Books*, June 6, 1968: October 10, 1968; November 21, 1968; March 13, 1969.

Fader, Daniel, *Hooked on Books*. New York, Berkley, paperback, 1968.

Featherstone, Joseph, "The Primary School Revolution in Britain." *The New Republic*, August 10, 1967; September 2, 1967; September 9, 1967 (available as reprint).

Friedenberg, Edgar, *The Vanishing Adolescent*, Boston, Beacon, 1959; paperback, New York, Dell, 1962.

Grier, William H., and Cobbs. Price M., *Black Rage*, New York, Basic Books, 1969; London, Jonathan Cape, 1969.

Hentoff, Nat, *Our Children Are Dying*. New York, Viking, 1966, also paperback.

Herndon, James, *The Way It Spozed To Be*. New York, Simon and Schuster, 1968.

Holt, John. *How Children Learn*. London, Pitman, 1968; Penguin Books, 1970.

———, *How Children Fail*. London, Pitman, 1965: Penguin Books, 1969.

Kohl, Herbert, *36 Children*. London, Gollancz, 1968.

Kozol, Jonathan. *Death at an Early Age*. Penguin Books, 1968.

Martin, Peter, "The Open Truth and Fiery Vehemence of Youth" and "The Schools." *The Center Magazine*, a publication of the Center for the Study of Democratic Institutions, January, 1969.

Neill, A. S., *Summerhill*. New York, Hart, 1960: Penguin Books, 1968.

Weber, Julia, *My Country School Diary*. New York, Dell, 1969.

Human Psychology and Development

The following books in somewhat different ways explore, develop, and support the idea that there are strong constructive and positive growth forces and tendencies in human beings, and that the business of education must be to give them the maximum possibility for growth.

Fromm, Erich, *Man for Himself*. London, Routledge, 1949.

———, *Escape from Freedom*. New York, Holt, Rinehart and Winston, 1941: paperback, Avon, 1965.

———, *Towards a Psychology of Being*. New York, Van Nostrand, paperback, 1962.

May, Rollo, *Man's Search for Himself*. London, Allen & Unwin, 1953; New York, New American Library, 1967.

Rogers, Carl. *On Becoming a Person*. London, Constable, 1961.

Rosenthal, Robert, *Pygmalion in the Classroom*. New York, Holt, Rinehart and Winston, 1968.

ACKNOWLEDGMENTS

The author gratefully acknowledges the permission to reprint articles from the following sources:

"True Learning," from *Broadside 2,* Copyright © 1968, School Services Group, Inc., Dan Pinck and His Friends, Prudential Tower, Boston, Massachusetts.

"A Little Learning," from *The New York Review of Books,* April 14, 1966. Reprinted with permission from *The New York Review of Books.* Copyright © 1966, The New York Review.

"Schools Are Bad Places for Kids," from *The Saturday Evening Post,* February 8, 1969.

"The Fourth R—The Rat Race," from *The New York Times Magazine,* May 1, 1966. Copyright © 1966 by The New York Times Company. Reprinted by permission.

"Teachers Talk Too Much," originally published as "Do Teachers Talk Too Much?" from *The PTA Magazine,* October 1967. Copyright © 1967 by John Holt.

"The Tyranny of Testing," originally published as "John Holt on Testing," by Dan Pinck and His Friends, The 8 by 8 Press, Boston, Massachusetts, 1968. Copyright © 1968 by The 8 by 8 Press.

"Not So Golden Rule Days," from *The Center Magazine,* a publication of the Center for the Study of Democratic Institutions, July, 1968. Copyright © 1968 by John Holt.

"Making Children Hate Reading," originally published as "How Teachers Make Children Hate Reading," from *Redbook*, November, 1967. Copyright © 1967, 1968 by John Holt.

"Order and Disorder," originally published as "Letter to the Editor" in response to the article "Teaching in Harlem," by Alexander Sharp, *Yale Alumni Magazine*, April, 1968. Copyright © 1968 by John Holt.

"Teaching the Unteachable," originally published as the Introduction to *Teaching the Unteachable*, by Herbert Kohl, *The New York Review*, May, 1967. Reprinted with permission from *The New York Review of Books*. Copyright © 1967, The New York Review.

"Education for the Future," by John Holt, from *Social Policies for America in the Seventies*, edited by Robert Theobald. Copyright © 1968 by Doubleday & Company, Inc. Reprinted by permission of Doubleday & Company, Inc.

"Blackboard Bungle," from *Book Week*, October 31, 1965. Copyright © 1965, The Washington Post Company.

"Children in Prison," from *The New York Review of Books*, December 21, 1967. Reprinted with permission from *The New York Review of Books*. Copyright © 1967, The New York Review.

"Comic Truth on an Urgent Problem," from *Life*, March 1968. Copyright © 1968 by John Holt.

About the Author

John Holt was born in New York City on April 14, 1923. He was educated at a number of schools in the U.S. and at Le Posey in Switzerland (1935-6), after which he attended the Phillips Exeter Academy, graduating in 1939. He earned a B.S. degree in Industrial Administration at Yale in 1943. Following this he served in the Submarine service of the U.S. Navy until 1946. He then worked in various parts of the world government movement, finally as Executive Director of the New York State branch of the United Work Federalists. On returning to the U.S. in 1953 after traveling in Europe for a year, he taught fifth grade in various private schools in Colorado and Massachusetts.

In 1964, his book *How Children Fail* created an uproar with his observations that forcing children to learn makes them unnaturally self-conscious about learning and stifles children's initiative and creativity by making them focus on how to please the teachers and the schools with the answers they will reward best. His subsequent book, *How Children Learn* (1967), also became widely known. The two are still in print and together they have sold over a million and a half copies and have been translated into over 14 languages.

Holt went on to become a visiting lecturer at Harvard and Berkeley, but his tenure at both places was short-lived. He did not feel the school establishment was serious about change in the ways he wanted to go, such as changing the relationship of the child to the teacher and the school to the community. In 1985, John Holt died at the age of 62, having written 10 books that were very influential in the development of the homeschooling and unschooling movements, including the classic *Instead of Education: Ways to Help People Do Things Better.*

Sentient Publications, LLC publishes books on cultural creativity, experimental education, transformative spirituality, holistic health, new science, and ecology, approached from an integral viewpoint. Our authors are intensely interested in exploring the nature of life from fresh perspectives, addressing life's great questions, and fostering the full expression of the human potential. Sentient Publications' books arise from the spirit of inquiry and the richness of the inherent dialogue between writer and reader.

We are very interested in hearing from our readers. To direct suggestions or comments to us, or to be added to our mailing list, please contact:

SENTIENT PUBLICATIONS, LLC
1113 Spruce Street
Boulder, CO 80302
303.443.2188
contact@sentientpublications.com
www.sentientpublications.com